791.43   109112
Mar

Martin.
Hollywood's movie commandments.

The Library
Nazareth College of Rochester, N. Y.

The Literature of Cinema

ADVISORY EDITOR: **MARTIN S. DWORKIN**
INSTITUTE OF PHILOSOPHY AND POLITICS OF EDUCATION
TEACHER'S COLLEGE, COLUMBIA UNIVERSITY

THE LITERATURE OF CINEMA presents
a comprehensive selection from the multitude
of writings about cinema, rediscovering ma-
terials on its origins, history, theoretical principles and techniques, aesthetics, economics,
and effects on societies and individuals. Included are works of inherent, lasting merit
and others of primarily historical significance.
These provide essential resources for serious
study and critical enjoyment of the "magic
shadows" that became one of the decisive cultural forces of modern times.

NAZARETH COLLEGE LIBRARY

Hollywood's Movie Commandments

Olga J. Martin

DISCARDED

ARNO PRESS & THE NEW YORK TIMES

New York • 1970

Reprint Edition 1970 by Arno Press Inc.
Library of Congress Catalog Card Number: 77-124018
ISBN 0-405-01624-7
ISBN for complete set: 0-405-01600-X
Manufactured in the United States of America

791.43
mar

HOLLYWOOD'S MOVIE
COMMANDMENTS

HOLLYWOOD'S MOVIE COMMANDMENTS

A Handbook for
Motion Picture Writers and Reviewers

By

Olga J. Martin

*Former Secretary to Joseph I. Breen, Director
of the Production Code Administration of the
Association of Motion Picture Producers, Inc.*

THE H . W . WILSON COMPANY
NEW YORK - - NINETEEN HUNDRED THIRTY-SEVEN

Copyright 1937

by

The H. W. Wilson Company

Published April 1937
Printed in the United States of America

PREFACE

The movies have been on and off the front page since the Nickelodeon days. On that page, too, the battle between film producers and public groups has been raging from the day that marked the birth of the first "flickers" to the present talking motion picture. Hugh Walpole remarked in an article appearing in the *News Chronicle* of London, "The whole history of the films is, at the moment, I fancy, at a very exciting crisis." It is! He said, further, "What is badly needed at the moment is not a book written by some superior intelligence about the art of the films; nor a book full of personal anecdotes about the habits of the actors and actresses—we have plenty of these—but serious work from the inside, dealing with the facts of actual film life. . . ." Since 1934, when fifty million movie fans declared at the box-office what they wanted in screen entertainment, the motion picture industry has been guided by public taste rather than by its own conceptions of what is recreative. The Motion Picture Production Code, which is a Code of Ethics, and which is the product of this public demand, represents a cross-cut of public opinion in America. It is significant as a social document.

This book, based on facts gathered from the "inside," is intended to fill a definite need. The analysis of the Production Code given in subsequent chapters is intended to acquaint the screen writers and the public groups which have shown a decisive interest in the subject, with the social purpose and dramatic *modus operandi* of the Motion Picture Production Code. It provides the defi-

nite information on the Code which both writers and
reviewers have been asking for.

Only those facts which are needed for an analysis
of the basic story and the finished picture are dealt with
in the subsequent pages. Details of censorship and of
the Code which are of little concern to the writer or the
reviewer are not given, lest they confuse the larger issue.
Those regulations which have to do with the thesis and
theme of the story and which determine its morality and
its acceptability under the Code have been given primary
consideration. The reason for this is that the details
of a story can always be changed; but to change the
basic theme and thesis requires the writing of an entirely
different story. Consequently, unless the story happens
to be an epic or a classic, it is the custom of the studios
to reject it rather than to attempt to make such radical
revisions.

The chapters devoted to screen writing problems,
too, are intended to fulfill a need. As one writer remarked in one of the theological magazines not so long
ago, "We are exhorted and urged to write for the movies
because of our understanding of the ethics of conduct;
yet no one has told us how this can be done. How are
we to contact the studios? What must we do to make
our stories saleable?" These, as well as a number of
other questions, suggested by an extensive survey of the
inquiries which writers usually make concerning these
problems, are answered in this book, in the chapters
dealing with screen forms, copyrighting, and marketing
channels.

The moral element appears to have won the war for
decency in films, but the public must remain wide awake
to secure itself against a return of the abuses which
brought on the crisis. How is this to be accomplished?

In the words of an editorial in the *Motion Picture Herald,*
it can only be assured by "an unrelenting vigilance
against invasions of the purposes embodied in the Code."
A definite knowledge of the Code appears, then, to be
essential to those who would uphold its dictums. This
book intends to present such information to the many
influential public groups which have continually sought
a better understanding of the Code. The Code must
look for its continued support from the many organizations which have contributed to its development—from
the religious organizations; from women's clubs, parents'
and teachers' associations; from the Review Boards, the
Film Councils, and the Better Movie groups; and from
all the members comprising the Protestant, Catholic and
Jewish Character Building Agencies which have been
cooperating with the industry's self-regulatory efforts
thru the Greater New York Forum on Character-
Building.

The author acknowledges with sincere thanks the
assistance given by Margaret Sprague Carhart, Ph.D., of
the University of California at Los Angeles, who has
generously contributed her advice and suggestions concerning many aspects of the present study.

OLGA J. MARTIN

CONTENTS

THE MOVIES AND THE PUBLIC

SEX IN PICTURES

GENERAL PICTURE SUBJECTS

SCREEN WRITING PROBLEMS

APPENDICES

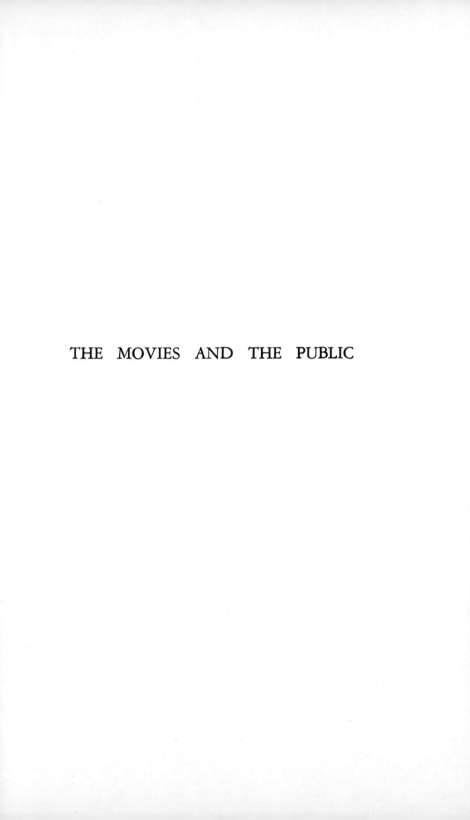

THE MOVIES AND THE PUBLIC

CHAPTER I

"A VERY EXCITING CRISIS"

In the traditional history of motion pictures, the dates 1889, when Thomas A. Edison invented the film camera, 1895 which marked the appearance of the first projection machine, and 1915, the year of the first "feature" picture, are recognized as landmarks. Few people, however, realize the importance of the date 1922 which marked the formation of the first trade association of the motion picture industry; namely, the Motion Picture Producers & Distributors of America, Inc. The abuses bringing this organization about may be inferred from the report made by the Cleveland Ohio Chamber of Commerce dealing with motion picture censorship:

"Early in 1922 the producers and distributors of motion pictures, realizing that the moral tone of their productions must be raised in order to retain continued public approval, organized an association known as the Motion Picture Producers & Distributors of America, Inc. The Hon. Will H. Hays, then Postmaster-General, resigned his portfolio in the Cabinet and became President of this new organization. Its purpose, as set forth in its Articles of Association is as follows:

'The object for which the corporation is to be created is to foster the common interests of those engaged in the motion picture industry in the United States, by establishing and maintaining the highest possible moral and artistic standards in motion picture production, by developing the educational as well as the entertainment value and the general usefulness of the motion picture, by diffusing accurate and reliable information with reference to the industry, by reforming abuses relative to the industry, by securing freedom from unjust or unlawful exactions, and by other lawful and proper means.'

"There has been evidence in the newspapers during the last few months, indicating that this new association sincerely and seriously intends to correct the evils which caused its organization. The pictures which are being produced this summer will be released in the autumn; the people will be able to judge at that time whether the efforts of the organization have been successful. For that reason further consideration of this report is postponed."

That same year the Federal Council of the Churches of Christ in America issued its first critical pronouncement against the motion picture industry in an article entitled, "The Motion Picture Problem," by Charles N. Lathrop.[1] Mr. Lathrop argued for a written definition of what constituted immorality in films and for some way of bringing pressure to bear upon the producers. Civic groups, he felt, differed too much among themselves to be effective; even the most intelligent members of groups conferring with producers had divergent opinions; and parents disagreed upon the films which might do harm to the morals of their children. Under such conditions, the only solution was some statement of principles to which the producers might be made to subscribe.

Mr. Lathrop's article gave, too, a comprehensive analysis of the censorship situation existing in the year in which the trade association commonly referred to as the "Hays Office" came into being. The mushroom growth of censor boards over the country was the first sign of an organized opposition against the film industry. It was the need for defending the industry against destruction by political and religious groups and other organizations which prompted the election of the Hon. Will H. Hays to the office as head of this association. Because of his political experience and his excellent personal reputation as an Elder of the Presbyterian Church,

---

[1] Reprinted on page 146 in *State Censorship of Motion Pictures* by J. R. Rutland (H. W. Wilson).

his selection as the head of the industry was highly approved by most factions.

Mr. Lathrop's article also calls attention to Mr. Hays' first efforts to clean up the industry by the adoption of the "Thirteen Points," which constituted a sort of "Gentleman's Agreement" between the trade association and the producers. These thirteen points were intended to exclude pictures which:

1) dealt with sex in an improper manner;
2) were based on white slavery;
3) made vice attractive;
4) exhibited nakedness;
5) had prolonged passionate love scenes;
6) were predominantly concerned with the underworld;
7) made gambling and drunkenness attractive;
8) might instruct the weak in methods of committing crime;
9) ridiculed public officials;
10) offended religious beliefs;
11) emphasized violence;
12) portrayed vulgar postures and gestures; and
13) used salacious subtitles or advertising.

Five years were destined to pass, however, before Mr. Hays realized that he needed more than a "Gentleman's Agreement" to enforce these points. In that five years the censor boards had continued to grow apace, and the "Thirteen Points" originally adopted required amplification to meet the ever-tightening standards of these censor boards. Consequently, in 1927, the trade association passed a resolution incorporating the thirteen points and new self-imposed regulations in a contract which was signed by all of the producers then members of the association. This Resolution of June 8, 1927, in substance, was as follows:

The Association of Motion Picture Producers, Inc., with the Motion Picture Producers & Distributors of America, Inc., resolved that since the sphere of influence of motion pictures had so widened and the standards of production so improved, they would adopt certain standards for the further improvement of films and for service to society. To accomplish these ends, they would exclude:

1) Profanity
2) Suggestive nudity
3) Illegal drug traffic
4) White slavery
5) Miscegenation
6) Venereal disease
7) Childbirth
8) Ridicule of the clergy
9) Willful offense to any nation, race, or creed.

They also resolved to use care in the treatment of such subjects as the Flag, international relations, religion, arson, use of firearms, all types of crime, brutality, Third Degree methods, capital punishment, sympathy for criminals, attitude toward public institutions, sedition, sex relations of any kind, surgical operations, use of drugs and law enforcement or enforcement officers. Seventeen studios signed the resolution, undertaking the responsibility of carrying out its provisions in good faith.

It is fair to say that the Producers' Association made sincere efforts to enforce its resolution. However, after three years had elapsed, it became apparent that the efforts of the association were inadequate to stem the tide of complaint by religious and other groups against immoral pictures.

The great moment of the struggle seemed to have arrived in 1930, when the groundwork was laid for an understanding between the industry and the public groups. The Producers' Association, determined to meet the public demand, conferred with numerous religious leaders to learn what reforms were desired. Since at that time the Catholic Church was at the forefront of the opposition forces, it was from this source that a plan came outlining the basic moral principles for the guidance of the motion picture industry.

These recommendations were taken under consideration by the Producers' Association. A reading of the Production Code will reveal that it has incorporated in it the original "Thirteen Points," the details of the 1927 "Resolution," and the basic moral principles suggested by the Catholic leaders, and urged upon the industry by the Protestant groups—and particularly by the Federal Council of the Churches of Christ in America which had been urging the adoption of similar measures since 1922.

The Code was prepared under the direction of the Hon. Will H. Hays with the counsel and guidance of leaders representing several branches of the motion picture industry. The task of formulating the Code was an enormous one, since it had to be so designed as to embody the basic principles of Christian morality without touching upon the theological beliefs of any one denomination. Mr. Hays' years of close contact with many religious leaders and public groups fitted him ideally for such a task.

The Production Code was written in a rather broad form of regulations which could be variously interpreted to apply to specific problems. This was a wise move for it provided the Code with the necessary flexibility to cover all issues and all situations which might reasonably be expected to arise in the consideration of story developments and film portrayals—a flexibility which would have been denied had the Code been written in such a form as to attempt to cover every contingency in advance. This form also suggested its eventual amendment thru the precedents which were to be set by its "test cases" in actual practice. Thus its basic law was designed to found its future interpretations upon precedent.

This 1930 Code incorporated the moral features which both Protestants and Catholics had been striving for, and, at the same time, satisfied the political censorship requirements. Its new moral principles had particular reference to story content and stressed the importance of the story's thesis in the moral evaluation of the finished picture. Eight years previously, Charles N. Lathrop of the Federal Council of Churches of Christ in America had urged the consideration of these very factors in his book on "The Motion Picture Problem" in which he advocated the adoption of such measures in these words:

"The scenario writing is a very important factor in determining the character of motion pictures. The producers have been severely criticized for spending so much money for star actors and actresses and so comparatively little on the preparation of their scenarios, thus not securing the services of the competent. The criticism of scenarios before production has been tried, but without much success. So much depends on the staging of the pictures and the details of acting that a picture may be made or marred in the production process. *However, the subjects treated and the personal standards . . . portrayed are important considerations.*"

Thus the gist of the changes incorporated in the industry's plan for self-regulation lay in the inclusion of moral principles for guidance in studying the morality of story content and thesis. The absence of these principles during the work of the trade association from 1922 to 1930 appears to have been responsible for the inability of the industry to satisfy public demand for morality. As is evident upon a reading of the "Thirteen Points," and the 1927 "Resolution," these were concerned primarily with the *details* of action and dialog rather than with a control of the philosophy inherent in the thesis of the basic story.

The motion picture industry in 1930 was at the crossroads. It was fully equipped for the realization of its object of self-regulation. It was in a position, for the first time in the history of the screen, to satisfy the public groups.

Yet, thus favorably equipped, and with a leader to urge them in the right direction, the producers defeated the efforts of their trade association. Consequently, the industry, in 1930, turned into a blind alley, at the end of which was chaos. In the ensuing turmoil the course of motion picture entertainment was destined to be violently changed; to be *forced* into new channels by outside agencies as an earthquake changes the course of a river.

The industry was on the threshold of its "exciting crisis."

CHAPTER II

A DECEPTIVE CALM

A period of deceptive calm followed the formulation of the Production Code. From 1930 to 1931 the press was more or less quiescent; the public groups expectant.

The Producers' Association appointed a Producer Appeals Board for the purpose of conferring on Code matters. This Board had the power of deciding whether the Code rulings were to be upheld or over-ruled in each specific case. The idea of the Board was adequate in itself, but it failed to take into consideration the economic considerations which would defeat the purpose of the Code. The round-table discussions which followed in the wake of each ruling made by the Production Code office, were too often settled in only one way. Producer A made it clear to Producer B that if Producer B would pass Producer A's picture now, producer A would pass producer B's picture when it came along. So changes demanded under the Production Code were frequently over-ruled and ignored.

Why did the producers thus ignore the Code? The reasons were many. Business men—whether they make pictures or other products—are traditionally conservative for the simple reason that change costs money. The producers were not at all sure that this new Production Code really represented what its public wanted. It was rather severe—or, at least, it seemed so in comparison with the very liberal literary standards of the studios at that time. Add to this the fact that as far back as time itself there has been warfare between the Church and the literary world whenever the latter overstepped the boundaries drawn by the standards of conduct set by the former, and it is easily seen that ready acquiescence to church pressure was not a response to be expected in the course of ordinary events. The producers felt that if the Code proved an impractical document, it would have to be so proved at the cost of thousands, and even hundreds of thousands of dollars. They were afraid that if stories were made to conform to the rigid standards set by the Code, the public might balk at seeing them—that it might refuse to accept preachments or Pollyanna philosophy with its amusement fare. For that is the light in which the producers regarded the Code at that time. Therefore they preferred to make few, if any, changes in an entertainment medium which was bringing them huge profits as it was. It was reasonable, in the face of this fact, to expect that the producers would hesitate to make changes suggested by the Code, even though Mr. Hays and the public groups were urging enforcement.

The response—or, rather, lack of response—of the movie audiences to the industry's few tentative attempts to make "clean" movies, did much, too, at that time to confirm the opinion of the producers that the Production Code was but a visionary document, not practically suited to the industry's problems, or the tastes of the movie audience.

Thus it was the age-old moral problem against the economic problem of the screen. What the producers failed to see, and what the public groups and Mr. Hays saw only too clearly, was that for the very reason that the motion picture was a medium of unprecedented emotional appeal and force, a change was not only necessary, but inevitable. Millions of young people were seeing the films, and, in the case of some pictures, at least, an immoral philosophy was being popularized thru this mighty medium. While there are no statistics as to the actual harm which these pictures did—along with contemporary literature advocating "liberal" standards— it is safe to assume that the young man and the young woman of the late twenties did not escape wholly un-scathed from the immoral propaganda of that period, of which the film represented one of the most potent and articulate forms.

That the Hays office itself felt at that time that the public groups were demanding more than was reasonable in reform is indicated by the former Governor Carl E. Milliken of Maine, Secretary of the Producers' Associa-tion in New York, in his remarks: "Since men differ in their interpretation of Holy Writ, there is no reason to expect that any form of entertainment, code or no code, self-disciplined or otherwise, will ever be free from criticism," and "It is inevitable that the Church should always have a higher standard than such a secular endeavor will perfectly attain." Governor Milliken's succinct reference to criticism is as true today as it was then. It is true, too, that at that period the demands of the Church were apparently far removed from the de-mands of the movie audience which seemed to prefer its pictures on the "liberal" side.

With this state of affairs existing, the only check to which the producers could be made to subscribe was that of "political" censorship—for the simple and economic reason that it would have cost money to ignore censorship requirements. To make changes in a picture after it was finished was extremely costly. Cutting out certain scenes and dialog could, more often than not, ruin the picture too—all of which meant loss to the producer. By living up to the censorship requirements, he could not only save himself the cost of retakes, but assure himself also of better box-office value by saving the vital parts of the picture from the censors' scissors.

Consequently, the Code was more or less ignored by the producers who generally over-ruled the efforts of the Production Code office to enforce its tenets, though censorship requirements were generally met.

The Producers' Association was functioning as a veritable clearing house for censorship information, so that the industry had at its fingertips the latest word in censorship deletions. In addition, the records of all censorship cuts went to the studios for their guidance. With these warning signals posted thruout the industry, and in the Association office, it was possible to foretell what scenes and dialog would conform to censorship requirements.

As proof that censorship alone was inadequate to satisfy the demands of the public groups, after a year of hopeful waiting the press broke out again with protests, complaints and tirades against the motion picture industry. The national assemblies of the Episcopalian, Presbyterian, Baptist, Methodist, Congregational and other churches passed resolutions condemning motion picture immorality. The *Christian Century* published a series of articles and editorials analyzing the effect of immoral movies on children and young people. Following this the Motion Picture Research Council inaugurated the Payne Fund Studies for the same purpose, conducted by the social scientists of seven leading American universities. Their findings provided the basis subsequently for the widely publicized book by Henry James Forman, entitled, *Our Movie Made Children* (N.Y. Macmillan, 1933).

It must be admitted that the critics had reason for complaint against the movies. Here are a few culled from the storm of protest in 1932:

"The advertisements are shameless enough," claimed the Reverend Clifford Gray Twombly, Rector of St. James' Church of Lancaster, Pa., and proceeded to prove his point by giving the following examples in his booklet *The Shamelessness of the Movies*: [1]

"Allow me . . . to present to you a list of some typical advertisements of the movies which have appeared in our own Lancaster newspapers . . . during the last three or four months:

'What does a travelling hubby do after he kisses his wife goodby?. . . Is a travelling husband entitled to a wife, and a sweetheart?'

'Social Secretary tells all. The bold facts, shocking but true. Reveals the private affairs of New York's fastest-stepping crowd of millionaires, from boudoirs to speak-easies.'

'Each kiss a new surrender, each woman a new affair. . . Women barred their doors, but gave him a secret key.'

'Alluring, pursued by many men. Experimenting with love, wild passions, gay parties. It tells who really pays for those ladies known as expensive.'"

This, however, said the Reverend Twombly, was not all, because the films themselves gave more "dirt" than was promised; and offers these examples:

"A man who had broken up a home and did not marry the woman afterwards, falls in love with another married woman and breaks up another home.

"Four lovers, two sets, one woman stealing the lover of the other woman, with subtle hints of all night hotel engagements."

With many more such examples, the writer concludes that the moving picture is one of the gravest menaces

[1] An Address delivered to the Women of the First Presbyterian Church of Lancaster, Pa., January 25, 1932.

the country has ever faced. He also tells that the *New Statesman* of London admonishes America to cease profaning herself by the "loathsome pictures that pour steadily from Hollywood." He also says:

"Again from London we hear that the America of the films would show a country in as lamentable a state as any nation ever suffered. A doctor writes in the *Journal* of the American Medical Association, 'There is no doubt that the American picture has become the school of delinquency.'"

From the Catholics, another warning comes. The Most Rev. John J. Cantwell writes in the *Ecclesiastical Review*:[2]

"Previous to the coming of the talking picture, the American-made motion picture sinned chiefly because of its vulgarity. . . . With the coming of the talking pictures has come greater and more far-reaching influence. The pictures now impress not only by sight but with animated sound as well.

"An examination of the number of motion pictures recently released . . . suggests that the entire motion picture industry has set itself to the task of seeing which company can produce the most vicious films."

After flaying the industry for the immoral philosophy taught and for the flippant Broadway playwrights whose stories are in part to blame for the final product, Archbishop Cantwell takes ten pictures selected at random, all of them offensive. One is based on seduction, rape and prostitution; another deals with aphrodisiac drugs, rape, and revenge; another is the story of a mother who becomes a prostitute in order to provide luxury for her son; in yet another adultery is justified. Archbishop Cantwell concludes his indictment with:

"It may well be sustained that 25 per cent of all pictures made in Hollywood in the course of a year are definitely bad and offensive."

[2] *Ecclesiastical Review*. February, 1934.

It is evident from the foregoing that censorship, with all of its cutting, did not improve the morals of the movies, and that if they were to be really reformed, the motion picture Production Code, providing control of the source material, would have to be enforced. The censoring of the objectionable product of 1932 with the object of purifying it was tantamount to the attempt to make an Arabian steed out of a jackass by cutting the latter's ears. It just couldn't be done.

This fact became apparent, too, to the Church leaders who had waited for three years to see the Code begin to function—during which interim the producer "Yes" game went forward with unabated zest.

There was another side to the problem, however, as is revealed by the press record of those who had a good word to say for the movies, in the summer of 1932.

TRENTON TIMES, September 19, 1932. "Fortunately the motion picture industry itself has been responding in recent months to the growing demand for less emphasis upon the sordid side of American civilization. There has been a noticeable increase in the number of screen productions designed to satisfy the most discriminating critic."

CHATTANOOGA NEWS. "A number of worth-while pictures which have appeared here lately . . . were indifferently patronized by the public. . . . We are weary of blaming movie producers for the tendency of movies toward filth and shabbiness. Obviously it is the public taste which needs elevating."

INDIANAPOLIS STAR. "Another service to the public as well as the motion picture industry itself has been rendered by the Motion Picture Producers & Distributors of America, Inc. . : . Will H. Hays . . . attacked 'hopped-up' advertising which emphasizes sex themes and other undesirable forms of press agentry at a gathering of executives. . . . The Hays organization in the past has shown its power to command the respect of the industry in fighting for higher moral and ethical codes."

PROFESSOR J. T. GRADY. "Motion pictures can and do inspire men and women to higher standards of life . . . nine out of ten people who see good pictures leave the theatre dwelling on the possibilities of betterment in their own homes, in their own speech and their own language."

GEORGE ADE. "The talking picture has become a member of the American home."

At the same time the Better Film Council and W. Ward Marsh of the *Cleveland Plain Dealer* pointed to a positive program for reform.

The opinion of both was that the hope of uplifting the standards of the screen lay in proving that good films were better business than bad, for no producer would deliberately choose to make objectionable pictures if good ones paid better. Not tirades from critics looking for evils, but education to make the public patronize the good films would be the plan of the Better Films Council. [3] W. Ward Marsh, the motion picture critic for the *Cleveland Plain Dealer* [4] put the whole matter succinctly:

"I have grown weary of the constant carping against the movies. Genuinely good ones too often are permitted to starve at the box-office.

"The elevation of the moral tone must come from within the industry, and it only comes in proportion to the demands set up by the public, not by the reformer, not by the constant clamoring minority, but by the public at large. . . ."

Dr. Fred Eastman, in a pamphlet entitled *Better Motion Pictures* (Pilgrim Press, 1936, Boston) admits that the churches, the schools, and the homes failed, in the past, to develop public taste. He says:

"This answer points an accusing finger directly at us. The element of truth in it strikes home. However, schools and churches are beginning to recognize more and more their responsibility at this point. Many schools have organized motion-picture appreciation classes. . . . In many churches Better Film Councils have been organized; church groups are cooperating with the local library in providing a reviewing service for the people of the community."

---

[3] Editorial account in Staten Island, N.Y. *Advance,* February 29, 1932.
[4] *Cleveland Plain Dealer,* March, 1932.

It appears from the records of 1930 to 1932 that the economic resistance of producers against the Code had its origin in the fact that dirt in the movies was proving "pay dirt" and that while but 25 per cent of the total product of the industry was on the sensationally smutty side, that 25 per cent was paying for the industry's losses on the clean 75 per cent which nobody seemed to support.

In answer to the claim made by producers that they were justified, because of the profit involved, in "giving the public what it wants," Dr. Fred Eastman states:

"To assume that church, school, and home bear the entire responsibility for the character of public taste . . . seems to disclaim any share of that responsibility for the motion pictures themselves. It intimates that the pictures exist to perform one function only: make profits. These assumptions are contrary to the facts. We have seen that the movies themselves are a school of manners, morals, and conduct, and that certain movie men admit it. They admit that they help teach the public to like what the movies like. *The development of discriminating public taste is part of the movies' job.*"

Other changes taking place, however, were to throw the balance in favor of the religious groups. Columbia's Vice President, Jack Cohen, probably disclosed the basic causative factor of the campaign against the movies when he said, "This violent burst of condemnation is directed *against something greater than the motion picture. . . .* The motion picture reflects the thing against which the Crusaders inveigh—*the tendencies of the times.*" The Depression had become a grim fact, and the pressure of the poverty which came in its wake was to dampen to a great extent the appeal of the "fleshpots." Hunger and terror and uncertainty turned thousands of people to the Churches for comfort. A more serious attitude toward life in general was but a natural reaction of the hard times. In this mood people were ready to listen to the exhortations of their religious leaders to return to Christian standards, to demand a higher level of entertainment. The time was ripe for a moral revolution. Thus 1932 to 1933 marked the era in which the pendulum was to begin its swing back to morality.

The denunciations against immorality found a bull's eye target in the current film fare. The movies with their heroes and heroines blithely "sowing wild oats" were suddenly "behind the times." To an impoverished country which had become religious and serious-minded, the sex attitudes of the post-war period became grotesquely unreal and antedated. The public at large wanted to forget its own derelections of the "gay twenties." The motion picture industry, on its last legs financially, was vulnerable to attack. The stage was set for the moral crusade.

CHAPTER III

THE LEGION OF DECENCY CAMPAIGN

In October, 1933, the first impetus was given to the birth of the Legion of Decency. The Most Rev. Amleto Giovanni Cicognani, Apostolic Delegate before the Charities Convention in New York, Archbishop of Laodicea in Phrygia, may be credited with having put the torch of religious fervor to the dry tinder of public disgust. The fire spread rapidly.

Hardly a month passed before an Episcopal Committee on Motion Pictures was appointed by the American Bishops at their annual meeting in Cincinnati of November, 1933. This Committee was composed of the Most Rev. John T. McNicholas, O.P., Archbishop of Cincinnati, Ohio (Chairman); the Most Rev. John J. Cantwell, Archbishop of Los Angeles, Calif.; the Most Rev. John F. Noll, Bishop of Fort Wayne, Ind.; and the Most Rev. Hugh C. Boyle, Bishop of Pittsburgh, Pa. That fall and winter the plans for a comprehensive campaign were carefully and painstakingly worked out. In April, 1934, this Committee declared war on the films thru the Legion of Decency, with its headquarters in New York City.

The far-reaching effect of the Legion of Decency boycott in which Protestant and Jewish groups joined, may be traced in the press reports of those days:

Catholic Boycott

CHICAGO DAILY TRIBUNE, June 5, 1934. "Urging that 'some censorship of morals' be put upon the motion picture industry,

Cardinal Mundelein formally brought the Chicago Diocese yesterday into the nation-wide fight now being waged by the Catholic Church against indecent films coming out of Hollywood."

Protestants Join

CHICAGO DAILY TRIBUNE, June 6, 1934. "Protestant leaders praised the leadership taken by Cardinal Mundelein. . . . They announced their delight in the broad form of the Catholic campaign in which, they said, Protestants, Catholics and Jews will be able to join wholeheartedly. . . ."

The accuracy of the prediction of united action may be judged by the press notices of the following month.

The Catholic drive had manifested itself in fifty dioceses. Some estimates placed the number who had signed the pledge of the Legion of Decency (which was a pledge to boycott offensive films) at 2,000,000, with every likelihood of a 5,000,000 total within a short time (NOTE: the total eventually reached 11,000,000 at the height of the campaign). In Massachusetts, plans for a specific boycott of indecent pictures by cooperation of 1,695,000 Catholics received the approval of the Archbishop of Boston, William Cardinal O'Connell. The Dallas Diocese joined the fight. Fifteen thousand members of the Holy Name Society pledged their support in San Pedro, Calif.

Dr. Harold G. Campbell, Superintendent of City Schools of New York City, ordered an immediate investigation of pictures shown to school children. Dr. M. E. Dodd, President of the Southern Baptist Convention, called upon 12,000 Baptist ministers to join the crusade. The committee of ten of the Chicago Church Foundation, a Protestant group, pledged cooperation. Support was ordered by the United Presbyterian Assembly, the Massachusetts Civic League, the Christian Endeavor Union, the Oregon Methodist Conference, and the National Conference of Jews and Christians.

The Legion of Decency boycott exerted an irresistible economic pressure. This pressure came at a time when the movie industry was practically bankrupt; when each ticket at the box-office counted in the balance. Millions of movie-goers no longer appeared at theatre box-offices, and thus it came about that the producers, again for economic reasons, were ready to accept the motion picture Production Code set up for the industry in 1930.

Things began to happen in Hollywood with amazing suddenness. On July 12, 1934, Will H. Hays and the Board of Directors of the Association of Motion Picture Producers, Inc., at Hollywood, concluded action amending and amplifying the Production Code Administration. The Production Code Administration came into vital being with a fighting Irishman, Joseph I. Breen, at its head. What his appointment meant may be gathered from press comments:

A Fighting Irishman Comes to Hollywood

TERRE HAUTE (Indiana) STAR, July 17, 1934. "Something is being done about it now out in Hollywood, be sure of that. Joe Breen, the two-fisted assistant to Mr. Hays, once of the Philadelphia *North American*, and at heart a good newspaper man, now has his coat off and what he is saying about what is fit and what is unfit for the screen carries a terrific punch to the cowering, found-out direction and script-writing ilk. For years they have been scoffing at the Hays rule. . . . Mr. Breen has been appointed umpire of the movies, assigned to preview every picture and to order the product cut, remade, or discarded. He will be guided by a code that for four years has been available to producers and accepted by them, but latterly regarded by many directors as irksome and in the way of progress and profit. . . . Smut, glossed vice, faked romance, unhealthy sex appeal, will not pass Joe Breen if he can spot them. He is that kind of an editor."

Under the new arrangement, the presidents of all the producing companies accepted full responsibility for pictures exhibited, and no company was to exhibit any picture not approved by the Production Code Administration, such approval being printed on the film.

The Producer Appeals Board was abolished. The notice of this change appeared in the trade paper *Variety* (Hollywood) on June 15, 1934:

"Producers' Appeals Board is abolished. Joe Breen is supreme pontiff of picture morals from now on. Only appeal from Breen ruling is to the Hays directorate in New York.

"This is the unanimous dictum of the major companies after long sessions in the Hays office deliberating over means to satisfy church pressure.

". . . Switch of all moral problems from the West to the East is revealed to have been motivated by an understanding that the crusaders have lost patience with the studio heads, but still believe in the judgment and good intentions of the Eastern executives. Inference is also being broadly drawn that there will be comparatively few reversals of Breen's future judgment. Haysites tonight describe Breen as in a position where his word from now on will be the industry's law. . . ."

Said Mr. Hays, as this new control emerged out of the war waged on the films:

"It is recognized that the solution of the problem of the right kind of screen entertainment rests solely with the quality of the product and these strengthened arrangements are directed to discharging that responsibility more effectively."

With all of these radical changes going into effect, the Bishops decided to give the industry one more chance to fulfill its promises of Code enforcement, and, pending further action by the Hays office, called off the boycott on June 21, 1934, just two and one-half months after it went into effect.

In conference with the Bishops were Mr. Breen and Mr. Martin Quigley who convinced the Episcopal Committee, under the leadership of Bishop McNicholas that the new machinery for control would function effectively. The Committee expressed its confidence, thru the press, in these words:

"The Episcopal Committee views with favor the renewed efforts of the organized industry to discharge its responsibility of issuing only such motion pictures as may conform with reasonable moral standards. The Committee believes that the Production Code, if given enforcement, will materially and constructively influence the character of screen entertainment. Hence it is disposed to render encouragement and cooperation to these efforts which it hopes will achieve the promised results."—*Los Angeles Times,* June 22, 1934

The Protestant groups, too, expressed their willingness to give Mr. Breen a chance to show what he could do. Dr. Worth M. Tippy, Secretary of the Church and Social Service Department of the Federal Council of the Churches of Christ in America stated in a press comment:

"The future of this decency drive, so far as Protestants are concerned, can be determined only by what takes place at Hollywood. If Mr. Breen succeeds and the producers support him, and what is done is not a temporary effect, there will be no more drastic action. We would like to see Mr. Breen succeed."—Hollywood *Citizen-News,* July 26, 1934.

The Federal Council expressed confidence in Breen's ability to raise film standards to the level demanded by the churches.

This time there was no back-sliding by the industry. A slip at that time would have meant its annihilation. That the efforts of Joseph I. Breen exceeded the hopes of everyone concerned, and that the Production Code was an effective instrument, is markedly apparent from a statement appearing in *Harrison's Reports* (a trade paper devoted to the interests of exhibitors), on December 15, 1934 by Pete Harrison known in the industry as one of its most outspoken gentlemen.   Said Mr. Harrison:

"In the last few months the moral tone of pictures has improved to an almost unbelievable degree. Along with the moral tone, *there has been a great improvement also in their entertainment values.*

"The person who is responsible for this improvement is none other than Joseph I. Breen, the unofficial representative of the self-regulated censorship system which has been adopted by the producers as the result of the pressure brought on the industry by the Legion of Decency. The obscenity that was found in four out of five pictures before last June has disappeared in the pictures that have been released since August.

". . . Since July 15th he has approved 217 pictures; 176 of these were passed by the censorship boards throughout the country without eliminations. Compare this record with the record prior to July of this year and you will realize the improvement that has been made in the moral tone of the pictures in so short a time."

At this point it is interesting to observe that there were no reversals of Mr. Breen's decision by the Board of Directors in New York on the few occasions in which an appeal from the Code ruling was made. It is also of interest to observe that the entertainment value of pictures has increased with the continued enforcement of the Production Code.

Further evidence of complete satisfaction with the work of the Production Code Administration appeared in the *Brooklyn Tablet* of March 16, 1935 indicating that the good work was continuing. In this statement issued by the Most Reverend John T. McNicholas, the Episcopal Committee on Motion Pictures took the opportunity to express its gratification for the marked improvement in

films, and to encourage all those who realize the menace
of immoral films to continue their vigilance so that the
ground gained might not be lost.

The final acclaim, however, came thru the Encyclical
on Motion Pictures, published in the *Los Angeles Times*
on July 3, 1936, in which recognition of the success of
the Legion of Decency campaign was expressed by Pope
Pius XI in these words:

"It is an exceedingly great comfort to us to note the outstanding success of the crusade. Because of your vigilance and
because of the pressure which has been brought to bear by
public opinion, the motion picture has shown improvement from
the moral standpoint; crime and vice are portrayed less frequently; sin no longer is so openly approved or acclaimed; false
ideals of life no longer are presented in so flagrant a manner
to the impressionable minds of youth.

". . . In particular, you, venerable brethren of the United
States, will be able to insist with justice that the industry in
your country has recognized and accepted its responsibility before society."

The *Motion Picture Herald* recorded in an editorial
by Terry Ramsaye the significance of the Encyclical to
the motion picture industry, in its issue of July 11, 1936.
He says:

"Signal success in the greatest of the social adjustments of
the motion picture, achieved for it by the American industry in
its adoption of and operation under the Production Code, is recorded in terms destined to become historic in the encyclical
letter discussing the screen by Pope Pius XI.

"The encyclical was given to the press of the world from
Rome July 2, and is presented in full in its official English translation in this issue of *Motion Picture Herald. . . .*

"Within the motion picture industry, the encyclical is to be
seen as of significant recognition, and approval, of the Production Code adopted in March of 1930, concerning which the letter
observes:

'It is promised in this agreement that no film which
lowers the moral standard of spectators, which casts dis-

credit on natural or human law or arouses sympathy for
their violation will be produced.'

"And this judged by His Holiness as 'a wise and spontaneously taken decision'. . .

"In substance the organized American industry's system of
operation under the Production Code is held before the world
by Pope Pius as an example for study and guidance.

"It is not, however, to be gathered that there is any declaration of a state of perfection, and the encyclical sets forth to
the churchmen of the world, including the American Bishops
first addressed, the importance of an unrelenting vigilance against
invasions of the purposes embodied in the Code, and includes
provisions for the expression of the moral pressures indicated.
Provision for reviewing committees and the issuance of lists of
approved product, in the general manner of the Legion of
Decency operation, is indicated. . . .

"'Vigilant care' is the title of and are among the most
emphatic words of the encyclical."

The plea for "Vigilant care" is not voiced alone by
the Catholic groups. The Protestant groups, too, demand
continued vigilance. While they have confidence in the
Hays Office, they have no illusions regarding the ability
of that organization to enforce its self-regulatory measures unaided by forceful public opinion. As Dr. Fred
Eastman states in his pamphlet: [1]

"How long the present trend in pictures will last, no one
knows—probably only so long as public pressure lasts. The producers have not been converted. . . . When public pressure lets
up they may again flood their theaters with pictures that harm
character."

Dr. Eastman then goes on to suggest a program which
will assure the continuance of better pictures for the
future. In this connection he says:

". . . The effectiveness and permanence of Mr. Breen's
office depend upon public support. . . . It is equally essential that

[1] *Better Motion Pictures*, by Fred Eastman and Edward Ouellette
(Pilgrim Press, 1936, Boston)

the public be educated concerning the whole history and process of motion pictures and their social effects."

Here are some of the main points advocated by the Protestant groups:

1) Join the Legion of Decency by signing its pledge. Boycott bad pictures and continue to support the good ones.

2) Help your children select the pictures they see.

3) Cooperate with others throughout the country who are working in this cause.

4) Educate your community by providing for the holding of forums and discussions in civic and religious organizations.

The *Christian Century* and the Motion Picture Research Council also advocate federal control of motion picture distribution and booking, as an objective to insure better pictures. In regard to this question, Dr. Worth M. Tippy of the Federal Council of the Churches of Christ in America, made the statement, according to press reports, that the Federal Council would conduct no boycotts or censorships "except against unsatisfactory films." Dr. Tippy added, however, that "if this effort to clean up the screen proves futile, the industry can count upon a tremendous move for federal control which inevitably will include some form of censorship." [2]

The "very exciting crisis," anticipated by Hugh Walpole has, indeed, come. But it has not yet passed. The industry may have won its laurels, but the fight for decency has just begun in earnest. A new war is raging on the Western Front. . . .

---

[2] Hollywood *Citizen-News*, July 26, 1934.

CHAPTER IV

THE ANTI-DECENCY CAMPAIGN

There is opposition to the motion picture Production Code from many sectors. Critics sneer at it, and producers many times balk at its rigid requirements. The slightest weakening in any link of the chain which has been forged by the Production Code Administration may, therefore, bring revolt in the ranks.

That all producers do not yet understand the Production Code is apparent from an editorial appearing in the January, 1935, issue of the *Motion Picture Herald* wherein one of the younger producers was credited with commenting:

"Things like the Legion [of Decency] always come to an end, and it will be doubly so in the case of motion pictures when audiences are faced with a steady flow of saccharine material."

The pungent editorial rebuttal to this statement is worthy of note as it comes from a trade publication considered to be the "voice of the industry":

"We must turn back somewhat wearied, again to say that it would be well if in the New Year someone might find a way to get producers, even the young ones, to read the Production Code, and there to find, if they can, wherein and whereby and how, if any, the Code demands saccharinity of the screen."

Producers are being gradually educated into an understanding of the Production Code, though it is likely that even today many of them do not thoroly comprehend the real function of the Code.

The wide-spread anti-decency campaign which is being carried on today is engaging the serious thought of the Producers' Association and the public groups interested in the continuance of the industry's efforts at self-regulation.   In an article titled "A Claque for Decency," appearing in the August, 1936, issue of *The Acolyte,* the Reverend Dr. Edward S. Schwegler discusses the problem and, at the same time, suggests a solution.   He says:

"Throughout the short but distinctive era of Decency on the screen right down to the present moment, there has been a very insistent and insidious anti-decency campaign.   It comes for the most part, from the hoity-toity fraternity composed of newspaper and magazine critics, writers of syndicated Hollywood columns, directors of 'cinema guilds,' and the like.   A great many of these very superior persons have endeavored from the very beginning to overwhelm the Decency Legions, the Breen Office under Mr. Hays [the Production Code Administration] and the Production Code which is followed in adjudging the moral values of a picture, with every possible kind of sarcasm and ridicule."

As a matter of fact, Dr. Schwegler continues, these "smart alecks" try to hold that nothing artistic has come out of Hollywood since the enforcement of the Production Code; that the Producers' Association and Mr. Breen are a lot of fussy old maids, and the whole business of censoring pictures for grown-ups is an insulting and puerile undertaking.   Yet it was only because of the Production Code Administration that the play, "The Children's Hour," with its implication of sex perversion, was recast into a natural love story.   Many other examples could be mentioned.   If we want plays made over so that they are not objectionable from a moral standpoint, says Dr. Schwegler, we must do something about the "smart alecks" and something to support the Production Code. He believes that a national defense of decency carried on thru columns for that purpose in newspapers all over the country is the answer.

An example of the attitude of some of these critics is revealed in the editorial titled "Smut Lust," appearing in the *Motion Picture Herald* of April 11, 1936. This editorial represents, too, the type of defense which Dr. Schwegler recommends:

"Under the aromatic title of 'Back to Smut,' one Mr. ———— has contributed to a recent issue of a studio periodical published in Hollywood a curious and altogether remarkable denunciation of the forces of decency and the self-regulatory efforts and devices of the motion picture industry.

"Mr. ————'s expression is interesting in its contradictions, being a professed expression in behalf of the screen and being the while so much at variance with the policies and performances of the industry which has set up and subscribed to the Production Code Administration, including, conspicuously his current employers . . . on whose staff he is listed as a writer.

"The whole matter of what he has to say, to be sure, is important only in that it is an articulate and frank exposition of a certain minority state of mind in that community which can do the industry no good. He begins:

'This is in the nature of a confession. Not so long ago I had to work for a living. I was staff writer for a publication which sincerely advocated a moral clean-up of pictures. I was in direct communication with leaders of a great many reform groups throughout the country. . . . Now, three years later, they have won their fight. They have succeeded in saddling the motion picture industry with the most appalling set of rules ever devised for the emasculation of free expression. I was a dupe and most of them are fools. . . .'

"The glib Mr. ———— did not use any of the considerable space at his disposal to submit samples of the morè 'appalling rules' or to present any gory displays of emasculations resulting from the rules. Such exhibits would be necessary to support the indictment of the Production Code—which document, by the way, he does not directly mention. In fact, he directly mentions nobody, nothing—thereby avoiding any facts invasive of his theme.

"One can gather, however, from Mr. ——'s lively screed, by inference, what he deems to be 'free expression.'

"The idea of 'free expression' is revealed in his slogan-title, 'Back to Smut,' and apparently not so much for freedom as for profit because of his declaration:

'If the development of movies is to be on to Elsie Dinsmore or back to Smut, then I say by all means let's get back to Smut and be quick about it. It might be a good idea for producers to hold a round-robin and begin the retreat together, because I have a sinking suspicion that if one of them jumps the gun and beats the rest back to green pastures, he'll make enough money to buy his brothers out by Friday week. . . .'

"That's Mr. ——'s freedom. It may be added that if one could get the Broadway and Times Square concession for the vending of gold bricks, heroin and evesflesh, without hindrance, he also could make a lot of money—Smut money.

"It perhaps did not occur to Mr. ——, when he said in his 'confession' that he wrote for a clean-up 'because he had to make a living,' that the implications might also extend to some aspects of his current expressions, too. If he is now writing in behalf of Smut for the love of it, he's classified, and if he thinks he is doing it for hire, directly or indirectly, there's a name for that, too.

"If one must speak of Elsie Dinsmore, one also recalls 'Little Women,' in perhaps a kindred category, which, as we recall, did rather well.

"Meanwhile grosses on the competent product of the period, all produced under the ministrations of the Production Code, appear adequate.

"In fact, business has been so good that even Mr. —— seems to have been able to escape from the job where he says, 'I had to work for a living,' into the movies, where, one would assume from his context, things are different."

Another example of the ridicule which is heaped upon the industry is represented in an earlier editorial, which appeared in the *Motion Picture Herald* of December 7, 1935, refuting the fallacious statements of a columnist. Under the title of "What is 'Adult'?" the editor said:

"Something of the internal, lingering, diehard opposition of some factors of the Hollywood community to the self-regulatory measures of the Production Code find expression in references to it as 'censorship,' more often than not as 'Hays censorship.' These expressions are commonly behind hand and whispered, but now and then erupt in indiscreet public audibility. A typical manifestation recently appeared in the contributions of Mr. ——, who writes for the Los Angeles ——.

"Said Mr. —— in substance, there was something to be thankful for in that newsreels did not come under the 'Hays censorship' and that therefore in newsreels at least the screen might achieve 'adult' material.

"It so happens that since most of the affairs which the newsreels have occasion to record are public affairs, *a certain common decency* that pertains to the public tends to prevail. It also so happens that the men who make the newsreels are perhaps continuously more in contact with, and responsive to American *mores* than their confreres of the fiction industry under the pepper trees and palms. Anyway, the newsreels require little regulative attention. Apart from that it might be observed to Mr. ——, . . . that all of the newsreels are under the banner of signatories to the Production Code. It is the comment of his contemporaries in the Los Angeles newspaper field that his copy has to pass two editors—maybe a third is indicated.

"But that phrase 'adult entertainment' especially protrudes. Not a few other screen commentators, mostly erectile young blades, prate about it. Examination of the pratings inevitably reveals a confused state of mind that can not tell an adult from an adulterer.

"The tedious truth is that mostly what these yearning young contenders would have specially licensed for the 'adult' screen pertains to manifestations of adolescence, a toying exploration of matters that betrays immaturity, regardless of the age at which the manifestations appear. Much that passes for sophistication is most exactly unsophistication.

"The true sophisticate knows about it and is therefore not concerned. It is the itch of naiveté that wants to bathe in it.

"The screen could do with some adult commentators."

A few such gems of defense as represented in these two editorials if broadcast thruout the country in regular newspaper columns would speedily put an end to the anti-decency campaign.

In the words of Dr. Schwegler, "If we do not organize . . . some means of applauding, defending and explaining Decency, the opinion will grow stronger and stronger that the only significant and articulate critics of the films are the champions of *indecency*."

Another danger presents itself also, and it is one which usually attends reform; that is, the public groups watching for evils in the films may, by too much nagging, and interference, lose the sympathy of the movie-going public as well as the producers. The Reverend Gerard B. Donnelly, editor of the Catholic weekly, *America,* warns those who are grudging in their admission that the films have improved, in these words:

"If after a year of unprecedented cleanliness in their product they are still to be cursed, threatened, and boycotted by Catholic organizations and speakers, why should they continue at all in the difficult pursuit of virtue? If they are damned when they are clean as roundly as they were damned when they were dirty, what—they might reasonably ask themselves—is the use of reformation? And why not return to a codeless, censorless regime in which dirt pays handsome returns?"[1]

The same warning might well be given to the public at large, for the fanatic in an average audience may do as much harm as the "smart aleck" critic.

The organized groups should fight against the anti-decency campaign which seeks to put to naught the efforts of the industry towards self-regulation. Dr. Schwegler's recommendations in this regard are pertinent

---

[1] " 'Definitely Cleaner' Films." *America,* July 27, 1935.

to a realization of the goal for decency. The words of the "naggers" and the "ridiculers" must be refuted. A "Claque for Decency" is very much the need of the moment.

CHAPTER V

WHAT THE PUBLIC *REALLY* WANTS

"What does the movie public want?" is a question which every producer has asked himself. His deliberations, however, apparently failed to give him a reliable answer. While he was attempting to measure the public response by "hits" and "flops" the more practical-minded public leaders were urging the public *to speak for itself.*

When this question became a public issue, many claimed to know what the public wanted. The query "What does the movie public want?" elicited opinions from all sides. Press editorials exhorted that "The movie public wants wholesome pictures that portray the decent side of life." "The movie public," claimed religious leaders, "wants pictures that are moral and direct attention to correct standards of life." Quite a few dramatic critics and columnists who were considered the minutemen of their profession vociferously declared "The movie public wants realism in pictures, and not a lot of Pollyanna tripe," which, in their parlance meant that they thought the public preferred to see the "seamy" side of life. Extremist groups, on the other hand, advocated the prohibition of all stories dealing with the sins and foibles of mankind, which would have meant damming the very font of drama.

Who was right? Which group represented the wishes of the public?

Was it possible to please both realists and idealists? This perplexing question arose in the face of the producers' own problem—which was that the motion picture industry would face speedy economic annihilation if it merely pleased some of the people all of the time, or even all of the people just some of the time. Its goal, in order to survive, has always had to be that of pleasing the majority. Yet, how were they to determine what the *majority* wanted? Any answer which one might formulate to this question leads directly to the queries: *"Who is the movie public?"* and *"Why* do people go to the movies?"

Who Is the Movie Public?

The hue and cry against motion pictures brought into the limelight the "movie public." The movie-goer was for years content with his dissatisfactions on the premise that everyone but he constituted the public. And his forbearance with the poor tastes of the hypothetical groups did much towards fostering current fallacies about popular demand. He was first provoked into serious concern about his unintentional contribution to the entire system of dubious entertainment when called to account by his priest, his minister, and his social and public leaders for his uncritical attendance at the cinema. Heretofore he had believed it was the other fellow's tastes which were being satisfied by the movies, and not his own. When he was made to realize his responsibility for the wave of unclean films, to recognize that *he was the movie public* and that he had a personal vote in the selection of his community's film programs, he became a factor to be reckoned with.

Actually, John Public and Mrs. John Public were not elevated in a day from the anonymity of mere spectators to discerning and articulate critics. Startling as it may seem, Will H. Hays, the generalissimo of the motion picture industry himself had a hand in this transformation. His was a vision which saw beyond temporary financial gain to the wider social view. Over a laborious sixteen years he assiduously fostered the organization of community previewing groups for the express purpose of creating a public *demand* for better pictures. From 1922 to 1930 these reached the gratifying number of three thousand. The impetus given by his original groups resulted in the establishment of thousands more in every part of the United States. The educational work of these groups was largely responsible for making public leaders "screen conscious," and for arousing the interest and concern of religious and social authorities which led to the memorable and unforgettable year of 1934 when the public, at the behest of its leaders, delivered its first ultimatum.

Thus the question *"Who* is the movie public?" was answered by the public itself in the past three years with a staggering slap at the box-office. Up to that time the opinions as to the class of patron which might be considered representative of the movie audience were widely divergent. The decision was final, however, when the "representative audience" demonstrated its majority by disastrously reducing financial returns on questionable films.

This revelation discounted the popular illusion that the modern stage play or the sophisticated novel typified the sort of drama the movie public wanted. This consensus of opinion, particularly as it was recorded in "red ink" statistics, convinced the producers that the time had come to elevate the drama to the level demanded by the fiercely articulate majority. But some of the present-day screen critics, blind to popular demand and tastes, are still crying in the much-maligned name of "art" and "freedom of expression" for the type of drama against which the movie public rebelled.

Actually, how many screen patrons demand "sophisticated" pictures? The critics who pretend to speak in their behalf overlook the fact that the demand for this type of drama emanates from a minority group far removed from the general movie public. In fact, the devotees of sophistry probably represent the advocates of the modern stage and not the audience of the motion picture theatre and, therefore, present no criterion of popular taste. It is understandable, of course, that those whose income places them in a position of security have less need of—and hence are less insistent upon—an idealistic philosophy in the entertainment afforded either by the theatre or popular literature. Perhaps it is for this reason, among others, that this class of audience favors the sophisticated novel and stage play which deal so extensively with the problems of sex, crime, and poverty "in the raw."

A factor which makes pardonable the dramatization of the sordid side of life on the legitimate stage is the preponderance of attendance by the mature adult, and the infrequent attendance by the impressionable youth, the adolescent and the child. The sophisticated drama undoubtedly has a definite place in the field of entertainment, but that place is not in the motion picture theatre— the sphere of *family* entertainment.

Taking into consideration both the urban and rural sections of the entire country, it has been found that the average business and professional man and woman, the high school and college student, the merchant, the tradesman, and the independent, serious-minded man and woman of the soil in our far-flung agricultural domain, constitute the largest part of the "movie audience."

These are the people who regularly or occasionally go to church, and who observe the normal standards of decency. It has been proved that a picture *must* appeal to these folk in both the large and small communities of the nation in order to be a box-office hit. The returns from the first-run houses alone would not pay more than the cost of the picture. The receipts from the neighborhood and small community theatres are an important factor, therefore, in determining the profit or loss on a film production. Consequently, serious consideration must be given to the likes and dislikes of this greatest part of the movie audience.

Why People Go to the Movies

Every member of the family, from grandpa and grandma down to the kindergarten tot, goes to the movies for the sheer fun he gets out of it. However, if one is to believe an eminent Swiss social authority, he gets more than that out of it! Theodore Reh, M.D., internationally known head of the Bureau d'Hygiène of Geneva, Switzerland, famous for his social studies, praises knowingly the social-hygienic effect of the movies. In an interview with the European representative of the *Motion Picture Monthly,* Dr. Reh makes the movies sound like a sort of safety valve for the family. He is quoted as saying:

"We have found that the motion picture is one of the readiest and best methods of transporting a harassed or jaded man or woman out of his or her disturbed personal atmosphere into an atmosphere of self-forgetfulness. . . . This tendency of the film is observable even in those motion pictures of which the story is, considered itself, depressing—found, at least, so long as the depressing theme is not one touching the real life of the spectator—for, at any rate, he concerns himself, while witnessing it, over other troubles than his own. On the whole,

however, no matter what there may be said from the point of
view of certain artists and critics, from the point of view of the
physician an optimistic film theme, if it is convincing, is prefer-
able to a theme that is pessimistic. Here is one reason why the
American film—generally hopeful, or, at all events, generally
leading up to a cheerful ending—is to be preferred to the too
often depressing screen stories of European production."

The American audience in particular demands a
"cheerful ending" in answer to a deeply-felt human
need for a kindly philosophy of life—the kind of home-
spun philosophy which made Will Rogers and Marie
Dressler the greatest and most beloved idols the screen
has ever known. Naturally, both grownups and young-
sters thrill to the vicarious adventure and the excitement
afforded by the romantic or adventure film. Of this
wholesome type little need be said. In the more serious
dramas dealing with social and ethical problems, the
movie-goer sees on the screen, more often than not,
people like himself, working out the problems of daily
living, working, and loving, to an ideal solution. Because
of its optimistic philosophy, even if the picture touches
upon his own troubles, the movie-goer is likely to be
refreshed, rather than wearied by the portrayal, and,
possibly, even find in it the encouragement to face his
own problems with greater confidence and fortitude.

To see a motion picture for the fun of it—to relax—
to forget the troubles of one's workaday world—to be
transported out of oneself—any one of these is a good
enough reason in itself to explain "Why people go to
the movies."

What Does the Movie Public Want?

Returning to our original question, "What does the
movie public want?" the following editorial comments

NAZARETH COLLEGE LIBRARY

appear to verify the conclusions in the foregoing analysis
and to suggest an answer:

The Dayton, Ohio, *Herald* believes that: "Pictures
exemplifying the decency of the average American home
and depicting the average American life have proved to
be popular without pandering to sex, sensationalism,
blood and thunder. . . ."

The Detroit, Michigan, *News* says: "There has been
no lack of appreciation . . . of pictures exemplifying
the decency and wholesomeness which characterize the
private life of the great majority of the American
people. . . ."

And the *Ladies' Home Journal* supports this appeal
for wholesome stories in these words: "The major plea
is for clean, virile pictures 'that bring out right ways of
living and thinking, illustrating the ideals parents and
teachers are trying to teach.' Clean plays. Better plays.
Good educational features on manufacturing, industry,
animal life. Stories of the lives of great men and women.
Travel and adventure pictures. These are what our cor-
respondents call for. . . ."

What the Public Goes to See

There is one way of determining with certainty what
the public wants, and that is by analyzing the support
which they have given to pictures in the past few years.
The pictures chosen as the "Ten Best" [1] by the critics
and the "Box Office Champions" [2] representing the
money-making pictures for the years 1930 to 1935 are
of interest in this connection:

In the selection of the "Ten Best Pictures" of each
year, the *Film Daily Year Book* states that "Critics

---

[1] "Best Ten Pictures" appearing in *The Film Daily Year Book* of
1936.
[2] "Box Office Champions" appearing in *The Box Office Check-Up
of 1935* (Quigley Publishing Company).

and motion picture editors of leading newspapers, magazines and trade papers thruout the country comprise the roll of voters."

The *Box Office Check-Up of 1935* states that the pictures representing the money-makers are chosen in this way: "The annual box office champions are pictures that did the highest amount of business during their entire run. Rankings are based on box office figures published in *Motion Picture Herald.*"

Here is the record for 1930 to 1935:

TEN BEST PICTURES	BOX OFFICE CHAMPIONS
1930 and 1931	[3] 1930 and 1931:
All Quiet on the Western Front	Cimmaron
Abraham Lincoln	Hell's Angels
Holiday	Trader Horn
Journey's End	Check and Double Check
Anna Christie	City Lights
The Big House	Min and Bill
With Byrd at the South Pole	Little Caesar
The Divorcee	Strangers May Kiss
Hell's Angels	Reducing
Old English	Daddy Long Legs
	The Man Who Came Back
	Politics
	Morocco
Cimmarron	A Connecticut Yankee
Street Scene	Animal Crackers
Skippy	
Bad Girl	
Min and Bill	
Front Page	
Five Star Final	
City Lights	
A Free Soul	
Sin of Madelon Claudet	

[3] Covers period of September 1, 1930 to August 1, 1931.

TEN BEST PICTURES	BOX OFFICE CHAMPIONS
1932	**1932**
Grand Hotel	Grand Hotel
The Champ	Emma
Arrowsmith	Dr. Jekyll and Mr. Hyde
The Guardsman	Mata Hari
Smilin' Through	Delicious
Dr. Jekyll and Mr. Hyde	The Man Who Played God
Emma	Hell Divers
Bill of Divorcement	One Hour With You
Back Street	Shanghai Express
Scarface	Arrowsmith
	Shopworn
	Business and Pleasure
	Tarzan the Ape Man
	Bring 'Em Back Alive
	Frankenstein
1933	**1933**
Cavalcade	I'm No Angel
42nd Street	Cavalcade
Private Life of Henry VIII	Gold Diggers of 1933
Lady For a Day	42nd Street
State Fair	Be Mine Tonight
A Farewell to Arms	Tugboat Annie
She Done Him Wrong	State Fair
I Am a Fugitive From a Chain Gang	Maedchen in Uniform
Maedchen in Uniform	Rasputin and the Empress
Rasputin and the Empress	Animal Kingdom
	The Kid From Spain
	Private Life of Henry VIII
1934	**1934**
The Barretts of Wimpole Street	The House of Rothschild
The House of Rothschild	It Happened One Night
It Happened One Night	Wonder Bar
One Night of Love	Roman Scandals
Little Women	One Night of Love
The Thin Man	The Gay Divorcee
	Dinner at Eight

Ten Best Pictures	Box Office Champions
1934—*Continued*	1934—*Continued*
Viva, Villa	Belle of the Nineties
Dinner at Eight	Riptide
The Count of Monte Cristo	Little Women
Berkeley Square	Dames
	Chained
	Judge Priest
	Sons of the Desert
	The Barretts of Wimpole Street
	Queen Christina
	Girl of the Limberlost
	Design For Living
	She Loves Me Not
	Flying Down to Rio
	The Lost Patrol
	Son of Kong
	Kentucky Kernels
1935	1935 [4]
David Copperfield	Mutiny On the Bounty
The Lives of a Bengal Lancer	Top Hat
The Informer	Roberta
Naughty Marietta	Midsummer Night's Dream
Les Miserables	Steamboat 'Round the Bend
Ruggles of Red Gap	David Copperfield
Top Hat	The Lives of a Bengal Lancer
Broadway Melody of 1936	She Married Her Boss
Roberta	Forsaking All Others
Anna Karenina	China Seas
	Goin' to Town
	Les Miserables

Reviewing the critics' "Ten Best Pictures" of these years, it is obvious that the choice of the critics was not always the choice of the public, as represented by

[4] 1936-37 *International Motion Picture Almanac* (Quigley Publications, New York City, N.Y.)

the Box Office Champions. Further, it is evident that the critics selected a number of pictures which would not at the present date meet the requirements of the Production Code. It is well to bear in mind, in analyzing the selection of the critics, that critics have always tended to place their stamp of approval upon pictures which they term "fearless," "virile," and "raw slices of life." This basis of judgment explains many of their selections for classification as the "Ten Best Pictures."

An analysis of the money-making pictures—the Box Office Champions—seems to indicate conclusively that the public goes to the theatre to see its favorite stars, giving little or no thought to the vehicle in which they may appear. Thruout the list of Box Office Champions it is evident that Will Rogers, Joan Crawford, Greta Garbo, Ann Harding, Marlene Dietrich and others have been the chief drawing stars.

It is obvious that the public does not allow itself to be influenced greatly by what the critics say, else these lists would be more in agreement than they are.

It is further evident that the public seems to like a certain number of musicals each year.

In view of the fact that for 1935, both the critics' list and the box office list appear to be, in the main, in agreement, the conclusion suggests itself that the critics may be trying to base their reactions upon the preferences of the average motion picture patron; or, possibly, that many of the critics are basing their opinions on the popularity of pictures in sections other than their own. The third conclusion which suggests itself is that in the absence of cinematic "raw slices of life," the judgment of the critics has had to be based upon other values in the pictures, and, that, for this reason, their choice coincides more closely with that of the movie-going public.

The Public's Mandate

The analysis of the box office reports by the editor of the *Box Office Check-Up* provides the final answer to the question which we have raised. This is what Martin Quigley has to say:

"The Box Office Check-Up is intended to disclose guidance upon that single question which . . . overshadows all others; namely, the relative box office values of types and kinds of pictures. . . .

"Striking is the essential character of those pictures which month in and month out stand at the head of the Box Office Champions. Since August, 1934, the following are among the subjects in this classification: 'Treasure Island,' 'The Barretts of Wimpole Street,' 'Flirtation Walk,' 'David Copperfield,' 'Roberta,' 'Love Me Forever,' 'Curley Top' and 'Top Hat.' Among these subjects which appear in the second position in these several monthly classifications are: 'Handy Andy,' 'Judge Priest,' 'One Night of Love,' 'Bright Eyes,' 'The Little Minister,' 'Lives of a Bengal Lancer,' 'Ruggles of Red Gap,' 'Life Begins at Forty,' 'Naughty Marietta,' 'Oil for the Lamps of China,' and 'Steam Boat 'Round the Bend.'

"This imposing group of attractions, each one of which has commanded world-wide audiences of vast millions, answers in thundering tones the dominant question of the theatre, which is, 'What Does the Public Want?' If we are to take this list for our guidance, which indeed we must, the lesson which it very obviously teaches is that the public wants decent, wholesome entertainment; that it most certainly does not want smut, sophisticated or crude, blatant sex or criminal glorification.

"The public obviously is not afraid of a classic of literature if it is sufficiently well-done, nor of a genuinely intelligent dramatic story. Its preference is plain for the handsomely staged, tuneful musical play. The simple and homely, when they are done with talent and sincerity, are in very genuine demand. The adventure story reasserts its time-honored appeal.

"Although the inescapable mandate of all this is sufficiently plain and emphatic, there is even further evidence to be gleaned from the record. It is to be found in *Motion Picture Herald's* list of the Biggest Money Making Stars of the year. . . . Standing at the head of this great list is the little child who during the past year has led countless millions to the doors of the theatres of the world—Shirley Temple. This little star's wholesomeness, simplicity and charm are the screen's attributes at its best. Next in the list is the revered Will Rogers, whose characteristics, so well known to the whole public, give enduring emphasis to the mandate covering what the public wants."

The ten best, and biggest money-making stars of 1934-35, to which Mr. Quigley makes reference in his article, are Shirley Temple, Will Rogers, Clark Gable, Fred Astaire and Ginger Rogers, Joan Crawford, Claudette Colbert, Dick Powell, Wallace Beery, Joe E. Brown and James Cagney.

In conclusion it is evident from the response of picture patrons, as summarized in the preceding pages, that the real "movie public" is that great majority of reasonableminded men and women in all communities whose standard of good taste can be relied upon to uphold ideals and yet concede the right to treat the problems of everyday life with a realism within the bounds of decency. For, after all, *decency is a part of everyday life.*

CHAPTER VI

THE PROGRESS OF DECENCY

The moral crusade, which, in 1934, reached the point of a drive for "clean movies," has forcibly advanced the standards of the modern cinema to embrace moral doctrines. Critics asserted that the two were incompatible, and that their union was an unrealizable ideal. They prophesied a diet of literary pap which would be more nauseating than smut. But they were wrong. 1935-36 saw the successful realization of an unprecedented and unhoped for ideal in motion picture entertainment—an accomplishment which has set a new cultural value on what may be the greatest moral agency of all time.

The transition from the post-war moral laxity and sex hysteria to the post-depression morality with its cry for "clean movies," did not, however, take place overnight. Behind it lies a long and stubborn history of moral revolt, well summarized in the report of the President's Research Committee on Social Trends presented in 1933:

"A study of interests and opinions reflected in leading magazines and allied sources in the United States since 1900 indicates the following as the most outstanding trends:

"Sexual irregularities, easy divorce and sex freedom in general have recently been approved to an extent entirely unprecedented in 1900-1905 in the channels studied. In magazine articles, challenges to traditional sex attitudes developed to a maximum between 1925 and 1928. In fiction, increased tolerance for violations of the monogomastic sex mores on the parts of heroines and heroes has been evident for all groups studied but especially for the 'intellectual' periodicals. The wave of approval for sex freedom appears to have been closely associated with the decline of religious sanctions for sex conduct."— *Recent Social Trends in the United States* (Page 411, Vol. I)

This report indicates the sort of material that flowed into the studios to be made into motion pictures. This is the sort of source material that comes into the studios today to be put thru various "cleaning-up" processes—to be properly laundered for the new-minded screen public.

Will H. Hays began his own private crusade as early as 1922 against this literary backwash-of-the-war which was flooding the studios. He banded together the dozen or so major companies in a "Gentleman's Agreement" to accept the social responsibility involved in entertaining millions of adults, adolescents, and children. He says of this period: "When in 1922 we set out deliberately to improve the social value of pictures, we faced the fact that we could achieve nothing by devoting our efforts solely to the creation of idealistic product." The only logical course seemed to be the development of local preview groups which should build up the demand in each community for better pictures. Within five years over three thousand such groups in the United States were functioning successfully to make articulate the demand for better pictures.

On the premise that there is "no order without regulation" Will H. Hays, after a five year rein-hold on the industry, put the backbone of a few decisive regulations into the "Gentleman's Agreement." These principles form the basis of the present much amplified "Production Code" of the industry. Today the Production Code Administration administers this "Production Code" with a hard paternal hand, and enforces it with the birch-rod of public opinion.

Will Hays was a good prophet when he said in 1931:

"A new era of entertainment progress is opening up for the motion picture screen. . . . The greatest of all censors—the American public—is beginning to vote thumbs down on the hard-boiled realism in literature and on the stage which marked the post-war period. . . . We have a new younger generation, now rising from the jazz age, that promises to support clean, high-purposed entertainment."

Consequently he was in a position to say "I told you so" when the 1933 report on Social Trends confirmed his opinions, and the Catholic Legion of Decency started the bonfire of protest that lighted the way for the moral crusade of 1934.

With a stiff code for self-regulation, and an extended experience in the art of literary laundering under twelve years of moral coaching by Will Hays, the industry was, like a well-trained understudy, ready for the public performance that the Legion of Decency demanded of it in 1934. And in 1935, the motion picture industry vindicated its splendid leadership.

Today the Production Code, which is moviedom's self-imposed "Ten Commandments," is the criterion by which all stories and pictures are judged. Not a single story is considered by the studios, which are members of the Association of Motion Picture Producers, Inc. and the leading independent producers, until it has been approved by the Production Code Administration. However, it should be remembered that, from time to time, an individual or a group of persons may produce a suggestive picture with the purpose of appealing to the few theatres thruout the country which cater to the sensationally minded of the community. An occasional foreign-made suggestive picture appears from time to time, also. However, both the domestically made and foreign importation of this class of picture constitute but a small fraction of 1 per centum of the total pictures produced and offered to the public in any year. When such pictures are objectionable, local ordinances against indecent exhibitions can and do meet the needs as to their control quite adequately if proper complaint is made to city officials. Such pictures either do not come to the Production Code Administration at all, or, if they do, they are rejected. In such a case, if the producer does not make the necessary changes to bring the picture within the provisions of the Production Code, he cannot secure the Production Code seal of approval for use on the title sheet of the picture. Exhibitors who are members of the Motion Picture Producers & Distributors of America, Inc., are pledged not to show pictures unless they bear the Production Code seal of approval, and, consequently, the exhibition of the rejected picture is limited to that extent.

We may say, therefore, that today—exclusive of the small fraction of 1 per centum referred to—all roads in the motion picture business lead to the motion picture "Production Code."

CHAPTER VII

THE BIRCH-ROD OF PUBLIC OPINION

The irresistible desire to imitate the other fellow—if he is successful—has brought into renewed use the birch-rod of public opinion upon the motion picture industry. In Hollywood they call the fever "popular demand," but the rest of the world calls it by its unadorned name—*cycles*.

The question no longer is asked "What do cycles do?" Hollywood knows. The present definition of a cycle is "a boomerang with the return hit usually out of the Hays office."

For example, the cycle of gangster pictures brought forth a public storm of protest which marked the birth of the "Crime Regulations" prohibiting the showing of gangster films; the immoderate drinking shown in almost every picture produced after the repeal of prohibition resulted in another public storm, with the subsequent edict from the Hays office that "Drinking must be reduced to the absolute minimum essential for proper plot motivation"; the public's revolt against the inordinate show of cruelty and the gruesome details of torture in a series of adventure and "horror" films, is responsible for the restraints placed on these subjects currently. All of these subsequently became "amendments" to the motion picture Production Code.

The origin, three years ago, of the Legion of Decency drive itself may be traced to the recurrent cycles of sex and gangster films in past years. When, a few years

ago, exhibitors all over the United States were asked in
a questionnaire sent out by *The Film Daily*: "What
complaints, if any, are voiced by your patrons?" they
made the almost unanimous and enlightening reply: "Too
many gang and sex pictures. Not enough diversity."
Most of the sex pictures dealt with the problems of
infidelity, adultery, illegitimate children, and deliberate
seduction. These and similar unsavory crime topics
represented as high as 50 per cent of the industry's
output in some past years. The enforcement of the
motion picture Production Code within the past three
years put an end to these questionable cycles. Will Hays
had been telling the industry for years that such pictures
should not be made. But no one paid attention to him
until the public itself revolted in 1934, at which time the
industry, in self-defense, gave him the power to enforce
the motion picture Production Code.

The British point of view in regard to cycles is
particularly interesting in that it expresses so clearly
the attitude of public-minded groups generally toward
questionable cycles. Sir Edward Shortt, President of the
British Board of Film Censors, makes this interesting
observation in his annual report:

> "I cannot believe that any *single* film can have any lasting
> effect on the public, but the result of the same theme *repeated
> over and over again,* might be most undesirable. Whilst this
> is so, I have always held the opinion that the film, within certain
> limits, must be allowed the same freedom as is accorded to
> other forms of dramatic art, always bearing in mind that it
> should be of a character which will not demoralize the public,
> extenuate crime or vice, or shock the just susceptibilities of any
> reasonably-minded section of the community."

The quantitative element does not in the ordinary
course of examination by the Production Code Administration enter into the consideration of pictures under

the Code inasmuch as judgment is based on each individual picture. The cycles, however, have served a good purpose in "high-lighting" incidents and phases in motion pictures which in lesser numbers might have gone unnoticed, and hence uncorrected. It is easy to understand that the incident and the phase that may appear unobjectionable in a single film might become offensive if it were repeated in a number of pictures.

The protests from women's clubs, from mothers all over the country, and from public and religious leaders against the excessive portrayal of drinking, brutality and gruesomeness, and against gangsterism empowered the Hays office to enlist public opinion to effect the enforcement to its full of the motion picture Production Code. So, while 1934 saw the enforcement of the *letter* of the Code, public opinion in 1935 may be credited with having made possible in full measure the fulfillment of the *spirit* of the Code.

CHAPTER VIII

"MOVIE-MADE" MORALS?

Will Durant states in *The Conditions of Civilization*:

"Through church, or family, or school, or otherwise, there must be a unifying moral code, some rules of the game of life acknowledged even by those who violate them, and giving to conduct some order and regularity, some direction and stimulus."

Sociological and psychological studies prove incontestably that morals are invariably "home-made." All the talk directed at "movie-made" morals has only tended to deflect the blame for family "black-sheeping" from the shades of Aunt Emma and Uncle Roscoe, et al, to the shoulders of the producers.

The Church, family, and school must always take the foremost place in teaching right conduct. The motion picture can never supplant or supersede them. It can unquestionably aid the work so begun by giving it stimulus; but it can no more attempt to *replace* this teaching than it could try to take the place of the schools in academic education. It has been the definitely affirmed objective of the motion picture industry to acknowledge a "unifying moral code" thru the medium of screen entertainment. A study of today's pictures will reveal that they stress the need for right conduct in such a favorable light that, when contrasted with the wrong conduct represented in a drama, the emphasis is on "good" and not on "evil."

Public Comments on Moral Influences of Movies

In this connection the comments of public groups on the moral influences of the movies are of interest. The following opinions were broadcast under the auspices of the Greater New York Forum on Character-Building, a cooperative project of Protestant, Catholic, and Jewish character-building agencies, including the Y. M. and Y.W.C.A.; Boy and Girl Scouts; Camp Fire Girls; Boys' Clubs; Settlement Houses; Junior Achievement; Children's Aid Society; Metropolitan League of Jewish Community Associations; and the Welfare Council.

"A very great improvement in moral tone and social values has been overwhelmingly apparent in motion pictures during the last year" (1935) was the assertion made by Professor Howard M. LeSourd, speaking over WEAF and a nation-wide network on a symposium "Character Building and the Screen."

Professor LeSourd, Dean of the Graduate School of Boston University, and Chairman of the Committee on Social Values in Motion Pictures, participated in the discussion with the Reverend Dr. Edward Roberts Moore, Director of Social Action of the Catholic Charities of the Diocese of New York and Secretary of the Council of the Legion of Decency, and Dr. William B. Millar, Executive Director of the Motion Picture Foundation of the U.S.A.

Describing the crusade of the Legion of Decency, Reverend Dr. Moore asserted that:

"Today the level of the nation's screen entertainment is immeasurably higher than it was before the crusade began. . . . Artistic standards have not suffered—quite the contrary. More people than ever are going to the pictures, so all are happy—the producers who feared the worst; the Legion which sees its objective—for the time, at least—attained; and the public which gets better entertainment."

Professor LeSourd attributed the improvement to a variety of reasons. He said:

"Whether the improvement be credited to self-discipline within the industry, to outside pressure of sincere and determined groups, to awakened public taste for better entertainment, or to all these factors, matters little—the improvement is here and should be taken advantage of."

All three speakers stressed the tremendous influence of the motion picture *industry* in the development of social attitudes and conduct.

In speaking of the social value in pictures, Professor LeSourd stated:

"Some of the most critical of the groups that preview and otherwise study the stream of motion picture product, are now variously reporting to their constituencies that from 95 per cent to 98 per cent of all entertainment pictures reaching the screen *contain neither episodes nor implications that are morally hurtful.*

"We cannot expect Hollywood to do more than to produce entertainment pictures that are wholesome. That is Hollywood's job. But the teachers and the religious leaders and the fathers and mothers of this country have a definite obligation in finding ways and means of seeing that the motion picture passing in constant stream before the eyes of our young people shall serve its maximum usefulness in stimulating thought and in the development of a keen sense of social values that shall prove to be of service in the development of our citizenship."

The editorial comment appearing in the March 7, 1936, issue of the *Motion Picture Herald* in regard to "The Parents' Job" emphasizes the conclusions in regard to the responsibility of parents which have been set forth in the statements of the Character-Building groups:

"With so many movements continuously beating the air with drives to make the movies safe for the young, etc., by special enactment of laws and assorted devices of censorship, there is pleasant re-statement of a sound contention in the utterances of Rabbi Lee J. Levinger of Columbus, Ohio, who wrote in the Sunday *Star* the other day:

'. . . it is merely mental laziness that makes most parents bewail the effect of the movies on their children, declaring that Hollywood is a debaucher of the young. Censorship, like charity, should begin at home. If the parent is really on the job, the movies will not hurt his child. In fact, instead of a curse, they may easily become a blessing.' "

CHAPTER IX

HOLLYWOOD'S "TEN COMMAND-MENTS"

A vast difference exists between a story that is "moral," and one that merely "moralizes." The misunderstanding current on this point accounts largely for the resistance of many modern writers to the efforts being made to reform literary standards. Obviously, a story that "moralizes," simply "dramatizes a sermon," and with this type of story an entertainment industry such as the motion pictures can have no more concern than the writer who shies from it. On the other hand, a "moral" story presents the problems of life as they exist in relation to society's legal statutes and "unwritten laws" governing conduct.

Styles in Morals

However, there are styles in morals just as there are styles in clothes, and one must distinguish between a spurious and an authentic code of morals. How is one to determine when a code of morals is authoritative?

Walter Lippman has clarified the meaning of morals thus: "An authoritative code of morals has force and effect *when it expresses the settled customs of a stable society.*" Stability, then, appears to be a factor to be considered in determining the authenticity of a code of morals. It is interesting to note this same factor of stability mentioned in an article in *Scribner's* by Eugene Lyons (former United Press correspondent in Russia) dealing with Russia's revival of decency, in which he says: "Outmoded sentiments like respect for parents, and gallantry toward women, neglected institutions like durable marriage, have been restored to official favor ..." and adds "The morality of guerilla warfare must give way to the *conventionalities of a stable society*."

Post-War Screen Morals

Speaking of the morals reflected on the screen, the late Andre Sennwald, former motion picture editor of the *New York Times* has been quoted as stating: "Very roughly speaking, the screen plunged from the unbridled ferocity and ethical imbecility of the war years into an extended orgy of sex during the swollen and comfortable decade that preceded the historic events of September, 1929. The sick and disillusioning years since then have created, perhaps, a new American temper. . . ."

Mr. Sennwald's statement may be interpreted to infer that the screen in recent years has been reflecting the "morals" of a decadent period. Obviously, the unsanctioned customs of this period were not the customs of a stable society, and, hence, did not represent an "authoritative code of morals."

One must differentiate between these unsanctioned customs and ethological standards in order to determine whether a story is moral or immoral in effect. Confusion has resulted in regard to moral standards because immorality has in itself been considered as a standard. In the war and post-war periods, with their total breakdown of morals, immorality was either condoned or ignored, depending upon the transient and confused mores of a particular time and place. The literature of that period (which also provided the screen material for current and subsequent years) reflected these erratic moral trends. But—and this is important—these temporary attitudes or customs were not, and never may be considered "moral." Broadly speaking, therefore, while a story may express the fluctuating so-called "morality" of a particular time and place, it may be immoral in its philosophy.

A Standard of Measure

Because of this confusion in regard to moral standards, the need arose of which Richard Dana Skinner, in his article "Morals of the Screen"[1] speaks in these words:

"Thousands, if not millions, of parents and teachers are trying to answer the question, 'Just what is an immoral or indecent screen play?' . . . Nothing is more obvious than the need of some *standard of measure* to determine the morality or immorality of the theme of a play."

The motion picture industry has had to choose a "standard of measure" which would be universally acceptable—a measure which would represent basic Christian standards. Strictly speaking, Christianity recognizes only one moral code—the moral law of the Decalogue. One of the first code of morals was given to the world in the Ten Commandments. The authoritative moral code of today is based on these same Commandments. Helen Hayes, in an editorial appearing in the August, 1936, issue of the *American Magazine* has pointed out their purpose in these words:

"The Ten Commandments presented basic rules of conduct to the world, not to stifle men and women, but to guide them toward a happier and more fruitful life. The Commandments were not imposed merely for the sake of directing others. Originally, I am certain, they were created out of much knowl-

---

[1] October, 1935, issue of *The Catholic Educational Review*

edge and a profound love of human beings, as principles for self-guidance. Before they became *a universal moral* code they were the tenets of a superior mode of living for men great enough to abide by their own rules."

The motion picture industry, in insisting upon "moral" themes, consequently has in mind at all times this "universal moral code" upon which each and every principle of Christian morality is predicated.

The idea of using a moral code for the regulation of an industry is quite an original one. It has never been done before. Society has its "unwritten laws"; the professional world has its "ethics"; the business world prides itself on its "square dealing"; the upright individual gratifies his sense of "fair-play"; and the devout man serenely practices the "Golden Rule." Whatever may be the measuring rod of his conscience, each man usually chooses according to his own concept of right. If he errs or deviates from the exact principle to which his group subscribes, it is (aside from the distinct criminal) usually done unwittingly. Consequently, because of individual differences in training, there is a wide diversity ordinarily found in the application of the moral and ethical standards of any particular group.

There is no diversity to be found in the application of the principles of the motion picture Production Code. Screen stories are not colored by individual conceptions of morality or ethics because every member of the industry must subscribe to a *written* Code, and, consequently, each portrayal is governed by exact principles.

Today the principles of the Production Code are used as the basis for the moral evaluation of all portrayals of life on the screen. As these portrayals are concerned with the problems encountered by men and women in all walks of life and the common incidents which test the moral fibre of the individual, the Production Code represents a significant social document. The consistent reflection of these principles in screen dramas must inevitably enrich the spectator's understanding of moral and ethical values and so contribute to individual and general welfare.

CHAPTER X

THE FACTS OF LIFE

The term "realism" as employed by certain members of the literary world, has always "covered a multitude of sins," but not so frequently has it represented "the facts of life." Under the pretext of realism the public has had served up to it the tidbits of juicy scandal, the rare and raw morsels of pornography, and the sweepings of the gutter in story and film fare.

But this is not intended as a plea against realism that *is* realism. The naughty but exciting things which warm the heart of the pornographic artist, and which he so loudly defends in the name of "art" and "freedom of expression," are but pale, neurotic ghosts compared with the actual facts of life. His "realism" is as far removed from reality as the sweet musings of an idealist, cloistered from the world.

The lovely ladies who languish in pink love nests, the "free soul" of the boudoirs, and the "modern" miss whose idea of being "broad-minded" is to be "sex-minded," the "strip-teasers," and the other gay and exciting members of this ilk romp thru stories without a hint of the kind of a world in which they are living. It is a very illusory world, indeed, inhabited by these care-free souls, and their paramours. Nothing ever happens to them except thrills, fun and whoopee! That is, on paper—or celluloid. But in real life it's quite different.

True realism in a story limns the conduct of its principals against the ethical background of the society in which these fictionized beings live. The reflection of the legal, social and ethical dictates of society are necessarily closely related to the lives of its members.

It would be false, for instance, to show unconventional conduct being condoned even in our modern age in an average Christian community. It is apparent even to those who do not make a study of sociology that unconventional conduct is not approved or condoned in such communities, and that the renegade from the ranks of the conventional has to face the condemnation and disgrace attendant upon such revolt.

Adultery

Our courts consider adultery as a violation of civil law; our Churches consider it a violation of the divine law. A "kept woman" or mistress is not accepted in decent society today any more than she was in days and periods of the past. Thus it is evident that while "times" may change, ethics do not.

The civil law from time immemorial has reflected the conservative thought. The ethics of the individual may diverge for a time from the accepted standard, but the ethics of the law are more or less stable. Thus adultery has been, and is today, the basis for a civil suit for divorce in every State of the union but one which recognizes no divorce (South Carolina). The law protects the estate of the innocent wife or husband against inheritance by the adulterous mate. If death of the innocent mate, for instance, occurs while the adulterous mate is illegally cohabiting with another, the guilty party may not inherit from the estate of the deceased.

The rights of the legal offspring, too, are protected against the claims of the illegitimate offspring which may be introduced into the family thru a wife's adultery.

Doubtful parentage may therefore deny inheritance of family property to a child.

The law, on the other hand, protects the child illegitimately conceived by giving the unmarried mother the right to sue for bastardry and support of the child, whether the father is married or single.

It would appear, then, that even in our very "modern" and liberal times, definite unpleasant consequences may ensue when adultery is committed, and this wrong-doing may cause grief to other lives, as well.

Seduction

In the matter of seduction which certain "modern-minded" individuals consider strictly as a personal matter of little consequence, let it be said that the law has very strict ideas of ethical and legal retribution for the commission of this wrong. Where a minor is involved, the act becomes a felony, and imprisonment of the seducer is probable if charges are filed against him. Even in the case of the seduction of an adult, the law seeks to protect the wronged individual. If the seducer is unmarried, the girl may demand marriage. If an illegitimate child is born, the woman may sue the seducer for bastardry and support of the child. These are the legal consequences.

The social consequences are even greater. Sociologists claim that the subsequent loss of reputation may be considered the greatest danger resulting from seduction. It has been found, from a record of many such cases, that the seducer usually goes about bragging of his "conquest" to his fellows, with the result that the girl is publicized as a "loose woman." But this is not the worst. The publicity given the wrong-doing by gossip or by public trial oftentimes results in solicitations for white slavery. This is particularly true in the case of young girls.

Where pregnancy occurs as a result of seduction, and abortion is resorted to, there is the danger of sterility or death, with consequent loss of a productive member to society. Where an illegitimate child is born, definite unpleasant consequences ensue, both economic and social, for the girl and the child. In addition, the very fact of pregnancy itself may bring future difficulties to the woman. The law in many States specifies that if it can be proved that an unmarried woman was pregnant before her marriage, (whether the pregnancy resulted in the birth of a child or not) the very fact of pregnancy—by a man other than the husband—may give the husband the right to request an annulment of the marriage unless he has had prior knowledge of the fact.

In the face of all this, it becomes evident that to dramatize wrong-doing as resulting in trouble to the wrong-doers is actually much closer to "reality" than the story which shows the individual living in an illusory world in which the law of cause and effect does not operate.

Illicit Sex

To come to that most disputed point in literature and in the movies—illicit sex—a few comments on the legal and social aspects of the question may be enlightening.

In most municipalities illicit sex is defined as a misdemeanor, and, if brought to the attention of the law, results in the arrest of the offenders on a "morals" charge. Imprisonment or fine is the penalty in some cases; but in any event, such a charge on the books of the police court is a disgrace to the individual. If the individual is brought into the morals court, the greatest danger resulting from such publicity is that the individuals may be tabbed by the underworld as "easy marks" for blackmail, prostitution, and the like.

Again, some marriage laws in certain States give the husband the right to demand annulment of the marriage on the basis of fraud if it can be proved that the wife has had illicit relationships prior to her marriage. A "morals" charge would definitely establish such proof. However, the law demands, too, that the complainant come with "clean hands," and therefore annulment may not be claimed if the complainant himself has been guilty of an illicit sex relationship with the defendant. If, however, the wife had become pregnant as a result of her earlier indiscretions, the husband could claim, upon proof, an annulment—unless he had been informed of the fact before his marriage.

It is evident from this that while modern ideas may be liberal, the law still abides by society's very conservative rules in judging conduct.

Divorce

If one were to believe what one reads in stories, it would appear that divorces are easily secured, and that if one of the married parties should get tired of marriage, all he or she needs to do is to ask for a divorce—and get it. That may seem to be the case in fiction. But truth is always stranger, and often much more severe, than fiction, particularly on the subject of divorce.

In many states a final decree for a divorce may not be secured in less than a year, and in some states in not less than three years after the filing of the first papers. Residence requirements vary from several weeks to five years, with, usually, a doubling of residence terms for non-residents desiring a divorce. Today there is a definite and concerted effort the country over to discredit and disqualify quick or easy divorces. The dangers of a quick divorce were exposed in an article appearing in

McCall's Magazine of May, 1936, by Richard A. Knight. He said that he told a client seeking a divorce:

> "If you take the advice you are paying me for, you will not go to Reno, nor Paris, nor Yucatan, nor any place where people are amiable about quick divorces. Because the divorce you would get would not be worth the paper it was written on. And your children by your subsequent bigamous marriage therefore could not possibly be legitimate."

Mr. Knight then goes on to state that it is the decision of the United States Supreme Court and all other jurisdictions that "The principle dominating the subject is that the marriage relation is so interwoven with public policy that the consent of the parties is impotent to dissolve it contrary to the law of the domicile." In further defining the meaning of "domicile," he offers the decision of a New York court:

> "The court finds that residence in a state solely for the purpose of obtaining a divorce is not sufficient to give jurisdiction to the court; that the defendant herein perpetrated a fraud upon the Nevada court in attempting to confer jurisdiction upon the court by false and spurious residence.
>
> "Bona fide permanent residence must be made of sterner stuff, and the courts of this state as well as of our sister states cannot be bound by proceedings so lightly regarded and decrees so founded."

It appears from all this that the resident of a particular state and a particular country is subject to the marriage and divorce laws of that country or state. If divorce is sought at all, it should be secured under the local jurisdiction to be free from contest. Otherwise the legality of a divorce may remain in question until tested.

Another fact usually overlooked in fiction is that no divorce is granted upon the plea of only one of the partners. The party securing a divorce must inform the other party of that fact by direct notice if that is possible, or, failing such direct notice, thru publication of a legal notice which has to run several weeks. The divorce is granted if no contest is made by the other party. But if the other party can prove that he or she was not informed of the divorce suit, and there is evidence that the information has been deliberately withheld, the divorce remains open to contest on the basis of a fraud.

All of these laws, and the long terms between the filing of the first papers and the issuance of the final decree have only one purpose—that of reconciliation between the estranged pair. It is notable that in those states requiring the longest time for the issuance of the final decree, there are fewer divorces, and more frequent reconciliations.

If relationship between the divorced pair occurs after the final decree has been granted, no recourse may be had to law. In the event of pregnancy, the birth would be considered as an illegitimate one exactly as if the pair had never been married. The woman could, of course, sue for support of the child on the charge of bastardry in such a case.

In view of these laws, it appears that the Code is not taking a "reformer's" viewpoint when it insists that divorce be indicated, not only as a serious step, but as one that is difficult of fulfillment and fraught with consequences. The social effects of divorce are treated also under the division dealing with this theme. The conclusion is that if the legal and social results of divorce were treated with truthful "realism" on the screen, they would in themselves constitute one of the strongest arguments against divorce.

Prostitution

Legally, prostitution is a misdemeanor. Its social effects are stated in no uncertain terms by one of our outstanding social authorities. In her book entitled *A History of the Family as a Social and Educational Institution,* Willystine Goodsell gives an account of the social effects of prostitution:

"Bad as is the institution in itself, its harmful effects were vastly increased when, in the twelfth century, it became the medium for the transmission of venereal diseases of a most virulent sort. From that century to the present, prostitution and venereal disease have gone hand in hand, the former serving as the chief dissemination of the latter. . . .

"The roots of the trouble are several. Ignorance of the facts of sexual life and hygiene, combined with lack of firm, sympathetic and intelligent training of boys in self-restraint, will, however, account for much of the social evil. But another cause may be found in society's double standard of moral conduct that makes a venial offence in the man what it harshly condemns in the woman. Until one standard of personal purity be held up for both sexes, until absolute monogamy be the ideal held before our youth from their boyhood, the evil, with its disintegrating effects upon family life, will not disappear from among us."

Conclusion

It appears that one does not have to go far afield to find sufficient realism in the consequences of the various sex problems treated under the Code. The consequences in themselves justify a serious treatment of these subjects. To ignore the legal and social effects of these evils would be false. Those who cry for "realism" should be able to take all of it, and not only that part which deals with the pleasures to be found in evil and ignores the unhappy results. Wrong-doing will always bring suffering in its wake so long as our society is so constituted that legally, socially and morally illicit sex relationships and easy divorce are condemned by our ethics of conduct.

MORAL VALUES IN PICTURES

CHAPTER XI

APPLICATIONS OF THE CODE

Almost every organized social group in the United States today is interested in a study of the motion picture, both with regard to its artistic and its moral values. Women's clubs, parents' and teachers' organizations, Churches, schools, colleges, and even business associations have joined in this universally popular pursuit. The screen undoubtedly is a new form of art and its symbolic language expressed thru the medium of film mechanics is a fascinating study in itself. Anyone who feels inclined to browse in its esthetic byways can go into any book shop for the latest treatise on the subject or attend the many art lectures dwelling upon this phase of the motion pictures.

The abstract subject of movie morals, however, has not thus practically been brought down to earth for examination. The very word "morals" connotes to the average person something rather vague, associated with the taboos and *verbotens* of "flaming youth." Its ethics are in an empyrean realm beyond the ordinary vision. Because of this, many people judge the morality of a picture by its "shock-ability"—by its proximity to the borderline of good taste; while others shrink from the screen dramatization of sin and crime, confusing the subject with the thesis. As a matter of fact, morality goes far beyond mere good taste and decency—the treatment of a story may satisfy all norms of good taste and decency and yet be shockingly immoral in its thesis;

contrariwise, a sin or a crime may be treated dramatically on the screen in a wholly moral and acceptable manner.

Screen Morals

Before one can fairly judge a picture's moral values, one must understand the moral principles applying to motion picture drama. The motion picture Production Code, by its written regulations, has helped to bring down to earth the principles of morality so that they can be understood by everyone. A study of this Production Code will provide the key to a study of the moral values of the screen.

First, let us define a few terms which are essential to any judgment of screen morals, and make certain distinctions which are necessary to an understanding of the applications of the Code. There is a difference between "theme," "thesis" and "plot"; between "immoral," and "indecent." The public and the scenario writer need to know all of these.

The theme of a play is simply the question put to the main character and the way he answers it. Thus the theme of *Macbeth*, say, is "Will you satisfy your ambition even if the obstacles demand your committing murder?" Macbeth's answer, of course, is "yes," and the theme of the play is concluded when his ambition proves his undoing. The theme, naturally, is most important to the moral value of a play, for the consequences of the character's answer determine such value.

The thesis is the philosophy of the play. The theme may be moral—that is, the wrong-doing may result in punishment or tragedy—and yet the general impression may be given that the misconduct is justified because it has brought enough temporary satisfaction to make it worth while. The play must have a moral philosophy as well as a moral theme.

The "plot" of the play is merely the sequence of action, and the complications. In itself it has little to do with the moral value of the play. The treatment which the incidents receive is the sole factor here—dialog and individual scenes may nullify the effect of an otherwise moral story.

What is an "immoral" story? It is one in which the actions held to be unethical by mankind in general are condoned or left unpunished. *Macbeth* is a moral play because Macbeth is punished for his murders and betrayals. Were he to live in splendor and happiness all his days, the play would be immoral.

The word "indecent," applied to motion pictures, is much milder in its connotation. It concerns the details of the story rather than the theme. It is a question of good taste and propriety based on long-established rules for human behavior. Richard Dana Skinner, in *Morals of the Screen*,[1] reduces classifications of bad pictures to the following:

1. The play is immoral in theme and indecent in in treatment.
2. The play is immoral in theme, altho inoffensive in treatment.
3. The play is moral in theme, but offensive or indecent in treatment.

As an illustration of both immoral theme and thesis, we may take excerpts from an article appearing in *America*[2] for October, 1932. The author writes:

"To take only films that have finished their run, let me point to 'Possessed' and 'Back Street,' two films which were among the most vicious of the past season. *They did not contain one objectionable line nor a single suggestive scene.* They were not

[1] October, 1935, issue of *The Catholic Educational Review.*
[2] "An Open Letter to Dr. Wingate" by Gerard B. Donnelly, S.J., in *America*, October 29, 1932.

designed as propaganda against established norms of conduct. *It is not the material that we condemn in these films, but the treatment; not the theme, but the thesis.* . . .

"Both films, you will recall, were stories of kept women. In each, the humanly appealing characteristics of hero and heroine were first emphasized very deftly so that strong audience sympathy was created in their favor. . . . A number of circumstances extenuating the sin were emphasized. In neither film did the real wife appear, and every other detail which might have shocked or antagonized the audience was carefully suppressed. The drawbacks of the guilty union were omitted or else cleverly used to give pathos to the story.

"*Finally the sin's immense rewards* in terms of human love and happiness were powerfully portrayed. In brief, the whole treatment of both stories was such that the audience was led to sympathize with the sinners and to approve their love completely.

"There, precisely, is the reason for our condemnation. *In persuading an audience to approve immoral conduct these dramas taught one of two false theses: The first was that adultery is not really wrong* if it brings great happiness to two likeable people. . . . *The second thesis was that even if adultery is really sinful,* the lovers would be fools to permit moral scruples to deprive them of happiness. . . .*"

In this same magazine, *America,* for August 10, 1935, an article called "Judging the Movies" [3] gives further insight into what constitutes an immoral picture:

"Now as *America* has so often and effectively insisted, all kinds of sin may be presented on the screen *if kept within the proper bounds and treated the right way.*

"The year's crop of pictures has often contained sin. 'There's Always Tomorrow' presented a husband secretly visiting his ex-secretary once a week; 'The Barretts of Wimpole Street' contained at least a suggestion of incest; 'We Live Again' portrayed the extremes of illicit relationship between two unmarried persons; 'The Hide-out' showed us a gangster powerfully tempted to do violence to an innocent girl; 'The Painted Veil' gave us a faithless and selfish wife, etc. *But in all these pictures vice was*

---

[3] "Judging the Movies" by Edward S. Schwegler, D.D., in *America,* August 10, 1935.

repelled as such, there was not too much offensive detail, and there was a reverent treatment of the opposite virtue. In short, the pictures were not demoralizing.

"On the contrary, one can say with reasonable certitude, that the opposite is true as regards some pictures. 'Side Street,' for instance, presented a married sailor who has affairs with two other women. The indecency of all this, though reprobated in the character of the wife, was so constantly held before the audience and presented with such nonchalance that to the clean-minded the film is disgusting, and to the more callous, funny. . . .

"As another example of a really demoralizing picture we may take 'The Gay Bride.' In this the heroine was ready to marry one after another of a racketeer gang, provided the new successor to her affections can promise her enough money. Though in the end she repented and married the only half-way decent member of the gang, the *utter venality of her character was so crudely insisted upon throughout most of the film that the thing became morally offensive.* There were, further, *several detailed scenes which alone would be sufficient to make the picture indecent.*"

The task of judging the movies, this author concludes, is no easy job, for the critic must consider both the way in which the action is portrayed, and the effect on the audience. He uses the word "indecency" to cover both morality of theme and treatment, with the following definition: "Indecency on the screen consists in lowering the moral standards of an audience whether by throwing its sympathy toward moral evil, or by . . . stressing details repulsive to moral sensibilities," and, according to the classifications of Mr. Skinner, the first would be immorality of theme, the second, indecent treatment.

Speaking of picture morality, Dr. Worth M. Tippy of the Federal Council of the Churches of Christ in America, says in his pamphlet, *How to Select and Judge Motion Pictures:*

"The deepest evil of the motion picture . . . . is the false and shallow concept of life which it is giving to our youth: ex-

travagant dress . . . constant drinking, silly and prolonged kissing . . . seduction as an art, suggestion in manifold sequences
that sex union may legitimately follow upon sex attraction without marriage."

An editorial appearing in a Protestant periodical [4]
gives its conception of what constitutes a moral picture
in these words:

"As the *Christian Century* interprets the mind of those who
are working for better pictures, they want much more than
decency. They want honest pictures. They want pictures which
do not lie about the true human values. . . Pictures which portray
us as we are, blundering, perhaps, but struggling toward a better
common life. . . Not propaganda; not preachy pictures, or sentimental ones. But strong drama with characters worth know-
ing. . ."

Inasmuch as the terms, "honest," and "true," are
used so frequently by certain groups in speaking of pictures, it is of interest to quote Clayton Hamilton's use of
these significant terms in defining picture morality.
Mr. Hamilton was at one time an editorial executive in
one of the largest studios in Hollywood. In an article
appearing some years ago he stated: [5]

"All philosophic critics are agreed that the morality or immorality of any story is dependent merely on its truth or falsity. . .
The one thing needful in order that a motion picture shall be
moral is that its makers shall maintain at every point a sane
and healthy insight into the soundness or unsoundness of the
motives and actions of the characters. The artist must know
when his characters are right and know when they are wrong
and must make clear to us the reasons for his judgment. He
cannot be immoral unless he is untrue. To make us pity his
characters when they are vile, or love them when they are
noxious, to invent excuses for them in situations where they
cannot be excused, to leave us satisfied when their baseness has
been unbetrayed, to make us wonder if after all the exception

⁴ *The Christian Century,* November 14, 1934.
⁵ Literary Review, N.Y. *Evening Post,* December 30, 1922.

is not greater than the rule—in a single word, to lie about his characters: this is . . . the one unpardonable sin."

Now with these definitions and examples from the writings of those who strongly influenced the Production Code, we may turn to the Code itself with a better understanding of its purpose.

Social Aspect of the Code

In indicating the application of the Code principles to different themes, the social significance of each regulation has been analyzed. A cursory reading of the Code is insufficient and likely to give a wrong impression of its value. For this reason, in subsequent chapters, the screen dramatization of the theme is analyzed in the light of each principle to the end that both the spirit and the letter of the Code may be understood.

Every rule and regulation of the Code has its origin in a definite social need, and is essential to a story which seeks to deal truthfully with life. The reader will find that an understanding of the moral principles and the social significance underlying each regulation of the Code will give him a better idea of the effect of screen stories upon motion picture audiences. This study therefore serves two purposes—to acquaint the reader with the moral aspects of the Production Code, and, at the same time, to acquaint him with the social factors and circumstances which have inspired the Code regulations and principles.

A review of the books and stage plays from which some of the outstanding pictures of the past two and a half years have been made will reveal the improvements which it is possible to introduce into a story by way of moral values. Take, for instance, the motion picture

"These Three," based upon the stage play, "The Children's Hour"; the film, "Anthony Adverse" based upon the novel of the same name; "Valiant is the Word for Carrie," adapted from the book of that title; "Anna Karenina," based on the Tolstoy novel; "Petticoat Fever," originally a play, to mention but a few screen adaptations. Some of this original material was changed in accordance with the Code provisions and the resultant screen plays were widely acclaimed as motion picture classics, morally sound and highly entertaining. They simply prove the entertainment value inherent in a moral approach to cinema problems.

The Writer's Viewpoint

The various groups mentioned are not alone in their interest in the Production Code. Writers and literary agents have sought diligently to understand the moral requirements of the screen with a practical eye toward the studio story market. An analysis of the practical applications of the Code will provide the needed information, not only to the motion picture study groups, but also to the writer interested in the screen market. In the latter category, if one is to believe statistics from the studios, the whole world—or, at least that part of it which can write English—is included. The subsequent chapters will treat with the Production Code from the writer's standpoint, since that is more comprehensive than a social study alone would be.

CHAPTER XII

THEMES SUITABLE FOR THE SCREEN

Before considering the Production Code regulations, the writer should study the definitions of a few terms frequently encountered in Code discussion.

The first of these concerns the *theme* of the story. The Code insists that the theme must be moral before the story can be basically acceptable for motion picture dramatization. The second concerns *"compensating moral values."* Certain themes may be *made* moral when such values are introduced. The third concerns *plot motivation.* Many subjects may be treated on the screen only when specifically required to provide the necessary motivation for the plot.

"Moral" and "Problem" Themes

The theme may be said to be "What the story is all about." The type of theme may easily be determined by asking a question about the story, and answering it. For instance: A woman is forced by circumstances to support herself—How does she do it? The answer might be:

1) By making a wealthy marriage;
2) By becoming a plastic surgeon;
3) By winning the sweepstakes;
4) By falling heir to an unexpected fortune;
5) By a spectacular resurrection of a Western "Ghost town";
6) By becoming an industrialist; etc.

If the problem put up to the leading character is answered in a normal and moral manner—according to accepted standards of conduct—the theme would automatically become morally acceptable under the Code and would not need to be subjected to the requirements of "compensating moral values," since, obviously, there would be no immoral or criminal action for which to compensate.   Such a story would be termed "moral."

On the other hand, this same question might be answered in any of the following ways, involving immoral or criminal actions:

1) By stealing another woman's husband;
2) By committing adultery;
3) By theft or robbery;
4) By marrying for the purpose of a quick divorce and alimony;
5) By becoming a murderess;
6) By becoming a prostitute; etc.

Immediately the story would become a "problem" story since it involves the *violation* of some civil, social, or moral law, and would, therefore, have to be subjected to the requirements of "problem themes."

Forbidden Themes

Certain themes are definitely forbidden for screen presentation.   Under this heading come all stories, themes and plots which for some reason or other do not permit the introduction of sufficient "compensating moral values" to counteract the evil they relate, or in any other way violate either the spirit or letter of the Code.   This includes those themes which do not technically come within the "problem" story classification, but which may present some phase or problem that may be judged subversive of the interests of society, or that may jeopardize the goodwill status of the motion picture industry.

Those listed below represent the type of themes forbidden by the Code:

CRIME

1. Arson may not be treated as a basic theme.
2. Gangster warfare and wholesale slaughter is forbidden.
3. Kidnaping of a child is forbidden.
4. The illegal drug traffic must never be presented.

SEX

1. Abortion or illegal operations, or any reference to them is forbidden.
2. Impotence may not be treated on the screen.
3. Incest or any reference to it is forbidden.
4. Miscegenation (sex relationships between the white and black races) is forbidden.
5. Sex hygiene and venereal diseases are not subjects for motion pictures.
6. Sex perversion of any kind is forbidden.
7. White slavery shall not be treated.

GENERAL

1. Nudism, or nudity may not be treated as a theme, or an incident in motion picture story development.
2. Racial or religious prejudices should never be made the basic theme of a screen story.

Allowable Themes

Any type of theme not within the category of those forbidden by the Production Code is acceptable for screen dramatization *if properly treated*—that is, its basic theme must be moral; its details of dialog, action, and locale must conform to the provisions of the Production Code, and its general treatment should be decent. Any "problem" theme requires, of course, the introduction of strong "compensating moral values."

Problem Themes

Any theme dealing with a problem—sex, crime, or social—must meet the following requirements:

1) It must be a theme allowable under the Code.
2) If allowable, it must have sufficient "compensating moral value" inherent in it to justify its treatment on the screen.

CHAPTER XIII

COMPENSATING MORAL VALUES

Any theme must contain at least sufficient good in the story to compensate for, and to counteract, any evil which it relates. While a theme may deal with immorality, its thesis must be moral. According to the Code, the usual compensating moral values in a story.are:

I. *The voice of morality*—as represented by good characters in the story—should provide the outspoken *condemnation* of the wrong-doing or evil. It should arouse sympathy for the right conduct and assure that the wrong conduct which is portrayed in the film is not condoned in speech or action by any character associated with the wrong-doer. The object of the "voice of morality" is to make articulate the moral principles involved in the issue which is being dramatized on the screen. It should always be voiced by likable characters with which the audience will sympathize. It should never be portrayed by characters giving any impression of hypocrisy, smugness, or blue-nosed severity. The object of the "voice of morality" is not to moralize, but to voice the fair and honorable side of the question or the problem, and to suggest its solution by means which would appeal to the fair-minded as the right and decent thing to do.

II. *Suffering.* Wrong-doing, whether intentional or unintentional, must be shown to bring suffering to the wrong-doer to establish the fact that it is inevitably painful, unpleasant, unprofitable and productive of unhappiness. Obviously, one cannot break the taboos of society and the moral laws without incurring the penalties associated with such lawbreaking. Suffering for wrongdoing may come thru many ways, i.e., self-condemnation, conscience, social ostracism, physical disability, legal retribution, personal loss, injury to a loved one, and so on.

III. *Reform and regeneration.* Reform and regeneration alone can be shown to cancel or pardon a sin or a wrong. Regeneration implies a desire on the part of the wrong-doer to do what is right. Not until there is evidence of repentance for the wrong which has been done, and a sincere effort is made to right the wrong, can the wrong-doer be shown to be relieved of the suffering which the wrong-doing has brought upon him.

IV. *Punishment and retribution.* Where a sin or a wrong is not forsaken, and the wrong-doer is not repentant, the story must indicate that some definite punishment ensues for the unregenerate character. The extent of the punishment naturally depends upon the wrong which has been done. Where a great injury has been done to another, the punishment would have to be commensurate to counter-balance the wrong.

Generally speaking, there are two classes of wrong-doers. In one class are those who deliberately and knowingly commit wrong because it is "easy," pleasurable, or expedient. In the other class are those who by faulty judgment or pressure of circumstances deviate from the moral principles to which they normally subscribe. In this latter class may be found those individuals who readily admit their mistakes and are willing to re-acknowledge their moral obligations. Once they realize the wrong which has been done, they are not likely to repeat the offense. Repentance and regeneration are more or less natural reactions when such characters discover that they have been guilty of violating a code of morals or ethics. In the former class, however, are the unregenerate characters who make no effort to correct their errors but continue in wrong-doing unaffected by the loss or injury their misdeeds bring to others. Repentance and regeneration would not be natural to such characters; and, therefore, the moral values of punishment and retribution are necessary to counterbalance the wrongs which they commit.

The Problem Theme

Having determined the basic moral values required to compensate for the depiction of crime or immorality on the screen, it is necessary to analyze how they may best be applied to the "problem story" theme. The theme states the problem which is put up to the leading character for solution. The way in which the character meets the problem determines whether the treatment of the theme of that particular story falls within the "problem" category. As stated in the previous chapter, if the character resorts to criminal, anti-social or immoral means to meet the problem, then the story is a "problem" story. To determine whether the theme is moral or immoral one must further analyze the story to see if the *consequences* required by the compensating moral values follow the wrongful actions.

The Problem Thesis

The compensating moral values require that not only the theme, but also, the thesis of a "problem" story must be moral. Therefore it is necessary further to analyze a story to determine the morality of the thesis.

If the story contains action or dialog which seems to *justify* the wrongful action of any character, the story is immoral in its thesis. If the story has in it any character who *condones* illicit sex relationships, irregularities, adultery, seduction, or crime, the thesis is immoral. If the story leaves the question of right and wrong unsettled, if it *leaves in doubt* whether these immoral actions are right or wrong, the thesis is basically immoral and the story is unacceptable under the Code.

To satisfy the requirements for a moral thesis, the Code requirement must be satisfied which reads:

> *"Evil and good are never to be confused* throughout the presentation."

In order to meet this provision of the Code, the further Regulations given below should be fulfilled:

1. Sin, crime or wrong must be definitely and *affirmatively* characterized as wrong;
2. They must not be condoned;
3. They must *not* be made to appear "right and acceptable";
4. *Audience sympathy must not be created* for the crime or sin (we may sympathize with the sinner—but not with his sin);
5. *The guilty must be punished.*

In addition the reasoning of the writer must be correct and moral, so that there will be no confusion of ethics in the solution of the problem. The entire prob-

lem of providing the proper solution may be summed up
in the words of the Code:

"The *motives* and *aims,* as well as the *means* employed, are
of first rate importance in the solution of problems.   It is not
satisfactory to arrive at the right solution for *wrong reasons.*"

To clarify the meaning of this regulation, a good
example is that of "The Sin of Madelon Claudet," in
which a mother had an admirable *aim and motive*—that
of providing education for her son—but sought to fulfill
it by *means* of prostituting herself.   Such a thesis is
immoral in that it appears to *justify* and to *condone*
prostitution; and, by choosing such an admirable motive
creates audience sympathy for the wrong (prostitution).

An example to explain the second point made by
this regulation is well represented by a story in which
the hero sought by various means to make the criminal
realize the evil of his actions.   He succeeded in doing so.
But his purpose, or reason, was not self-exposure for
the sake of regeneration, but, rather to frighten the
criminal into suicide to escape punishment.   Such a story
arrived at the right solution for wrong reasons; for there
was a total absence of regeneration or punishment; and
suicide in itself represented an immoral act since its
object was to escape punishment for wrong-doing.   The
attempt to make another individual commit suicide was
also wrong, representing murder by indirect methods.

In regard to "punishment" the Code definitely and
strictly "prohibits the subterfuge of attempting to wipe
out a protracted wrong by one last line of *dialog* affirm-
ing the right."   Dialog alone carries no conviction.   The
Code regulations state:

"Even though punished, the 'sin' or crime *must not be made
so attractive* that in the end the condemnation will be forgotten
and only the apparent joy of the sin will be remembered."

"Decent" Treatment

The factors mentioned so far have had to do with the "morality" of a story's theme and thesis. To meet the further requirements for "compensating moral values" the treatment of the story must also be decent. The Code states in this regard:

> "The location of scenes and the conduct, demeanor and attitude of the players enter very much into the question of the flavor of the appeal of the right or wrong presented."

A story may be entirely moral in its theme and thesis, but its moral effect on the audience would be entirely nullified if many of the scenes were to be played in dives, saloons, and bedrooms; and if the players' gestures and postures were suggestive and offensive; and, further, if the story were replete with vulgar, double-meaning dialog. A moral story could be made to have an immoral effect on the spectator by indecent treatment.

The same is true with regard to a story which had for its theme a "problem," and introduced the compensating moral values required under the Code, but thru indecent treatment of dialog and acting nullified the moral effect sought by means of the "voice of morality," suffering, reform and regeneration; or punishment and retribution.

Decent treatment, therefore, is also required to meet the provisions of the Production Code applying to stories of any kind.

Summarizing, the compensating moral values in a story may be said to be represented in the following elements:

1. The theme must be moral—the unhappy consequences of wrong-doing must be shown.

2. The thesis must be moral—the ethics of conduct must be made clear in the development of the plot, and situations.

3. The treatment must be decent—the action and dialog of the characters must be decent, and the atmosphere and locations of the drama must be wholesome.

Chapter XIV

PLOT MOTIVATION

The plot of the story is very often the part of the screen play which is likely to run counter to the Production Code provisions. A theme may be, in itself, perfectly moral, but if the plot is replete with offensive and unacceptable details, the entire story becomes unacceptable codewise.

A good example is the theme based on the thesis that "Crime does not pay." As it is developed in the gangster stories, however, with their details of crime, brutality and wholesale slaughter it is not acceptable. In this case, while the theme in itself is admirable, yet the plot requires so much offensive material in order to tell its story that the general effect of the picture, in spite of its moral theme, is undesirable.

Another example is a theme which might seek to establish that adultery is wrong and which develops its story by emphasizing all of the details incident to sex, passion and immorality. The details in such a story, rather than the theme, would be remembered and therefore it would have an immoral and unwholesome effect on the audience.

Those provisions of the Code which have particular application to plot are treated in the Second Section of the Code under "Principles of Plot."

Generally, the *details* of crime, and the *details* of sex are forbidden. Where it is possible to change these details and still to maintain unbroken the trend of the story, the plot can be dramatically treated under the Code. Where, however, these *details* are essential to the plot, and it is not possible to substitute some acceptable elements in their place, it is dramatically impossible to treat that particular plot under the Code. In such a case the *plot* itself would need to be changed.

CRIME IN PICTURES

CHAPTER XV

THE MOVIES AND CRIME

Referring to the crime wave, President Roosevelt stated:

"I ask citizens, individually and as organized groups to recognize the facts and meet them with courage and determination. . . . Law enforcement and gangster extermination cannot be made completely effective while a substantial part of the public looks with tolerance upon known criminals or applauds efforts to romanticize crime."

The United States has become crime conscious under the efficient regime of the "G-men." This consciousness has led to the critical appraisal of the influence of the movies upon crime. Consequently the Federal, state, and local law-enforcing agencies have all been instrumental in affecting the self-regulatory policies of the motion picture industry on the serious public question of how much of crime can be safely shown in pictures.

This powerful array of public forces has helped the Association of Motion Picture Producers to enforce its crime regulations. As a result, the details of crime no longer form the major portion of pictures as they did in pre-Code days.

There is little likelihood that the efforts of the industry on this score will be aborted. If any one producer is tempted to disregard the dictates of the Production Code Administration, his unapproved picture must still run the gauntlet of the state and municipal censor boards —and most of the latter are under the control of local Police Departments. Such a picture would be mercilessly cut by these censor boards, and what would be left would hardly be a saleable spectacle.

With all of the law-enforcing agencies cooperating with the efforts of the motion picture industry to take the glamour out of crime, the motion pictures have made worth while strides, and have become a potent force for law-enforcement.

In connection with the industry's self-regulatory efforts, the public statement issued by Peter J. Siccardi, Chief of the Bergen County Police, Hackensack, N.J., President of the International Association of Chiefs of Police, offers an interesting and enlightening commentary on the work of the Production Code Administration:

"At the last Annual Convention of our Association I was instructed by resolution to confer with leaders in the motion picture industry and to ascertain what steps, if any, were being taken by the makers of pictures to assure, first, that the screen should not be contributory to crime and, second, that the treatment of police characters and stories on the screen be handled in a true light.

"I was further instructed definitely to request of the picture industry that all stories dealing with crime be handled with recognition of the fact that the police problem is a continuing one, a vital one in the national war against crime and that we need the support and understanding of our communities. This very necessary relation might easily be disturbed by any practices in a great entertainment medium that might tend to portray our police personnel in an untrue light.

"For the past week (March 11, 1935) the industry has thrown open its doors completely to the survey I came here to make. The records have been made available to me and the present and future policies have been discussed with the utmost frankness. I have been allowed to sit in at actual conferences of the Production Code Administration, set up by Mr. Hays and operated here by Mr. Joseph I. Breen.

". . . On two points I have arrived at definite conviction:

1) The industry is conscientiously and painstakingly studying each crime story with a view to discouragement of crime rather than its encouragement.

2) There is an intent and a present practice thruout the workings of the Production Code Administration to make sure that the police officer is presented in his proper light.

"I have been agreeably surprised to find that the industry has gone much further in these regards than I had suspected. They have not been satisfied with a negative attitude but are keying all crime stories to emphasize the lesson that *crime does not pay*. As a police officer of many years' experience this seems to me a valuable contribution to crime prevention.

"The details and Code principles used in this attempt of the industry to cooperate with the forces of law and order are exhaustive and, in my opinion, largely effective.

"Prior to my visit to Hollywood I have for four months caused an investigation to be made in the field by twenty members of the police profession. These men have viewed the current pictures particularly with our problems in mind and they all report to me that there has been vast and steady improvement in the handling of crime themes. Only after arriving here did I understand the reasons for this progress.

"As President of the International Association of Chiefs of Police I wish to express my thanks to the industry both for its attitude and for its thorough spirit of cooperation with us."

CHAPTER XVI

THE CRIME REGULATIONS

The Production Code permits the treatment of crime on the screen in its statement, "Crimes against the law naturally occur in the course of film stories," but very definitely restricts its manner of dramatization in its various regulations. The Production Code Administration has clarified its interpretation of the crime regulations in these words:

"The Code recognizes crime as a constant concern of the human race and as something of immemorial interest to young and old; as a standard dramatic theme; and, consequently, as a fit subject for treatment on the screen.

"In laying down rules to govern the making of crime pictures, therefore, it is not the intention of the Code to prohibit or prevent the representation of criminals and their crimes, nor unduly to restrict in the treatment the true characterization of criminals and the portrayal of their deeds. For, after all, from the standpoint of dramatic balance, the hero's counterpart must be a true villain, and right must have as its contrary a true wrong; while from the standpoint of moral equity, there must be well established crime in order that just punishment may be inflicted.

"The intent of the Code is, rather, to insure above all that crime will be shown to be *wrong,* and that the criminal life will be loathed, and that the law will *at all times prevail.*"

Generally speaking, for the purpose of an analysis, the crime regulations contained in the Production Code may be classified as (1) the general provisions which govern the thesis or philosophy of the story; (2) the particular provisions relating to the specific attitude of the story towards law and law-enforcing officers; and (3) the general rules and amendments restricting the "details of crime."

Classification of Crimes

The Code classifies crimes within two separate categories; i.e., those crimes which are naturally repellent to an audience; and those crimes which are attractive because of the elements of heroism or glamour with which the criminal exploits are invested. It adjures that the former be restricted in their portrayal lest audiences become hardened to the thought and fact of crime; and that the latter be handled with extreme care to avoid romanticizing crime, or creating audience sympathy for the criminal's unlawful actions. The Code states in this connection that:

"1. Sin and evil enter into the story of human beings and hence in themselves are dramatic material.

"2. In the use of this material, it must be distinguished between sin (crime) which by its very nature *repels,* and sin which by its nature *attracts.*

"(a) In the first class (repellent crimes) come murder, most theft, most legal crimes, lying, hypocrisy, cruelty, etc.

"(b) In the second class (crimes which attract) come . . . crimes of apparent heroism, such as banditry, daring thefts, leadership in evil, organized crime, revenge, etc."

The Code then goes on to say that the danger inherent in the first class of crimes is that "people can become accustomed even to murder, cruelty, brutality and repellent crimes," especially those who are *young* and impressionable; and that the second class requires special care "as the response of human natures to their appeal is obvious."

The Thesis of the Crime Story

In addition to analyzing the types of crimes, the Production Code outlines the moral principles which must be followed in the development of the thesis. These principles are primarily concerned with proving the thesis that *crime does not pay*; that it is wrong, and that it brings suffering and punishment to the offender. In order to prove this thesis, the sympathy of the audience must, of course, be on the side of law and order. The Code states that:

"1. No plot theme should definitely side *with evil and against good.*

"2. No plot should be so constructed as to leave the question of *right or wrong in doubt or fogged.*

"3. No plot should by its treatment *throw the sympathy* of the audience with . . . crime, wrong-doing, or evil.

"4. No plot should present evil *alluringly.*"

Since the law must be shown triumphant in all crime stories, the thesis that crime does not pay is automatically proved. The foregoing principles, if applied to the story, will establish the fact that to commit a crime for any reason is *wrong*; and that criminal activities are not exciting and glamorous but productive of unhappiness to the offender.

The Story's Attitude Toward Law

Assuming that the thesis of the story is in accord with the Code principles, the specific attitude of the story towards law and law-enforcing agencies next comes under the test of the Code provisions.

The Code regulations require that the courts and the judiciary be portrayed with due respect for the integrity of the law. In other words, while an individual within the system of the law may be shown to be corrupt, the law in general should not be discredited by the action of a single individual. To assure that there will be no reflection upon the law or the law-enforcing agencies, the Code requires that the corrupt individual be apprehended and punished by law exactly as would be the criminal.

There is another precaution to be observed in a story dealing with crime—there must be no miscarriage of justice. Consequently, a story having as its theme the execution of an innocent man, or the incarceration of an innocent person in prison for the crimes of another, could not be permitted for the screen. There would, naturally, be no objection to the indication that an innocent man is threatened with such a fate, or is actually imprisoned for a period; but it would be necessary to show that the real culprit is eventually found and punished and the innocent person is freed.

A third precaution, under this same head, is that the law must never be shown to resort to unlawful means or methods to gain the ends of justice. If a law officer were to resort to crime in order to apprehend and punish a criminal, then the law officer would himself be a criminal. Obviously, the sympathy of the audience would be thrown against the law by such a portrayal. There is no room within the law for unlawful practices, and, consequently, under the dictates of the Code, any such suggestion in a screen story should be carefully avoided.

With this intent of the Code understood, the Production Code Administration has given the following interpretation to the principles relating to the treatment of the law in pictures:

RESPECT FOR LAW

On the general subject of respect for law, the Code states: "Law must not be belittled or ridiculed, nor must a sentiment be created *against* it."

This regulation has been applied in practice as follows:

(a)   Law and all lawful authority must be treated with respect in the widest sense of the word.

(b)   Nothing subversive of the fundamental law of the land, and of duly constituted authority, can be shown.   Communistic propaganda, for instance, is banned from the screen.

(c)   Law and justice must not, by the treatment they receive from criminals, be made to seem wrong and ridiculous.

(d)   Perjury, under any circumstances whatever, is wrong.

(e)   Riots and agitation inciting to public violence can be indicated only to the extent necessary for the purpose of plot development.

SYMPATHY FOR LAW

The Code regulation regarding sympathy is self-explanatory and needs no further amplification:

"The presentation of crimes against the law is often necessary for the carrying out of the plot.   But the presentation must not arouse sympathy *with* the criminal as *against* those who must punish crime."

LAW-ENFORCING OFFICERS AND AGENCIES

The Code regulation reading, "The *courts* of the land should not be presented as *unjust*" has been interpreted as follows:

(a)   High government officials must not be presented as untrue to their trust *without suffering the proper consequences.*

(b)   The judiciary and the machinery of criminal law must not be presented in such a way as to undermine faith in justice.   An individual judge, or district attorney, or jail warden may be shown to be corrupt, but there must be no reflection on the law in general, *and the offender must be punished.*

(c) The police must not be presented as incompetent, corrupt, cruel, or ridiculous in such a way as to belittle law-enforcing officers as a class.

PUNISHMENT

On the subject of punishment, the Code says:

"Crime need not always be punished so long as the audience is made to know that it is wrong."

This regulation has been interpreted by the Production Code Administration in this way:

(a) Whether there should be any punishment, and what the nature and extent of it should be, depends upon the character and magnitude of the offense.

(b) Sometimes suffering and *regeneration* alone satisfies all reasonable requirements of morals.

(c) In cases of flagrant public violation of the law, circumstances demand that the law be actually shown taking its course. In instances of minor violations, however, it is enough to show in a brief scene or in a few lines of dialog that the law is about to take its course, or that some other punishment is actually impending.

The Plot and Details of Crime

In order to meet the growing demands by the public and by law-enforcing agencies for a lessening of crime details in pictures, the Production Code Administration found it necessary to amplify its crime regulations. The original Code made the following provisions for the treatment of the plot and the details of crime in pictures:

"1. Criminals should not be made heroes, even if they are historical criminals.

"2. The treatment of crimes against the law must not make criminals seem heroic and justified.

"3. Methods of committing crime . . . should not be so explicit as to teach the audience how crime can be committed; that is, the film should not serve as a possible school in crime methods."

Further regulations of the Code for the treatment of crime are outlined in Appendix II, forbidding the presentation on the screen of the illegal drug traffic and the details of smuggling; and requiring that a minimum of detail be established in showing the technique of murder, brutal killings, and the methods of crime, particularly theft, robbery, safe-cracking, arson, dynamiting of trains, mines, buildings, etc.; the use of firearms is also restricted by these provisions; and the proper treatment of revenge is presented.

The amendments which amplified, and, in some cases, restated more specifically the original provisions of the Code are given in Appendix III in their actual form. For the purpose of this discussion, however, they are classified in this chapter separately under the headings of (a) Methods of committing crime; (b) Methods of preventing detection; (c) Methods of intimidation; (d) Use of weapons; (e) Murders and killings; and (f) Brutality and gruesomeness.

The Code not only requires that "details of crime must *never be shown*," but also states that "care should be exercised at all times *in discussing* such details." Generally speaking, the visual details and the discussion of methods of crime should never be so explicit as to teach how crimes can be committed.

(a)   METHODS OF COMMITTING CRIME

For instance, the details of the methods used by criminals to break into a house for the purpose of burglarizing it; the portrayal of a holdup; the graphic account of theft, shop-lifting, or pocket-picking; the suggestive picture of a kidnaping; the incendiary details of arson; the preparations and the minutiae for the execution of a murder; the instructive particulars for the use of poisons or drugs; the tools and detailed methods employed in safe-cracking—all these and innumerable other depictions of crime on the screen present details which are so explicit that they *teach* how to commit crime. Therefore they may not be introduced into a screen story. The only exception to the rule applying to "details of crime," is in the case where fantastic methods are employed which could not possibly be imitated, and where non-existent devices are used which could neither be procured on the market nor manufactured for criminal use.

(b)   METHODS OF PREVENTING DETECTION

The precautions used by criminals in avoiding detection should not be indicated in a screenplay. Details such as wiping off finger-prints or wearing gloves to avoid leaving finger-prints, and any other methods which are likely to suggest means of evading detection are forbidden for screen presentation. This type of instruction is considered definitely anti-social, since it constitutes, in effect, instruction in crime methods. There should be no discussion of such details.

(c)   METHODS OF INTIMIDATION

In accordance with the Code regulations which forbid the "flaunting of weapons by gangsters or other criminals," the screen story should not treat in detail with the methods used by the criminal to intimidate his victims. This means, literally, that the words, gestures and actions of the criminal and the reaction of his victim to threats and intimidation by means of violence should not be presented on the screen. To show in a picture how criminals can torture, bind up, or lock up their victims, is tantamount to instruction in criminal methods and these details are, therefore, forbidden in motion pictures. Where such action is important to the plot of the story, it can be suggested.

(d)   THE USE OF WEAPONS

In the words of the Code, "There must be no display, at any time, of machine guns, sub-machine guns, or other weapons generally classified as illegal, in the hands of gangsters or other criminals."

The excessive use of guns and of gunplay places a story in the "gangster" class and automatically disqualifies it under the Code for picturization. Guns should not be shown unless absolutely essential to the plot, and even then their use must be definitely restricted. Censor boards everywhere are becoming very strict in regard to the show of guns in motion pictures, for the reason that it suggests to potential criminals the power which weapons can give them over others, and how to defy the law.

(e)   MURDERS AND KILLINGS

The Code requires that "action showing the taking of human life is to be cut to the minimum." Therefore the following rules apply in crime stories:

1. Action suggestive of *wholesale slaughter* of human beings will not be allowed by criminals in conflict with the police; in any conflict between warring factions of criminals; or in public disorder of any kind.

2. Law-enforcing officers should not be shown *dying* at the hands of criminals. In this category are included private detectives, guards for banks, motor trucks, and any other servants of the government or private law-enforcing agencies.

3. Even where murders occur in mystery stories, they should be reduced to the minimum essential to the telling of the story. A series of murders should only be introduced where absolutely necessary for the plot. No murder should be obtruded into the story merely for the sake of "punch."

4. No details should be given in any story suggesting how a brutal murder or killing has been accomplished.

5. Suicide, as a solution of problems occurring in the development of screen drama, is to be discouraged as "morally questionable" and as "bad theatre"—unless absolutely necessary for the development of the plot.

(f) BRUTALITY AND GRUESOMENESS

Because of the distaste on the part of audiences everywhere against the gruesome details and the excessive brutality shown in many pictures of the past, the Code regulation that "Excessive horror and gruesomeness will not be permitted" is being enforced to its fullest extent. If it is necessary to the plot of the story to indicate brutality, it may be suggested in such a way that the audience is not subjected to its horror-provoking details. Censor boards are becoming increasingly strict about these particular elements in pictures both in this country and abroad.

While the regulation stated in this simple statement appears very innocuous on the surface, it has been responsible in the past two years for the decline of the out-and-out "horror" pictures of yesteryear. If it were not for this simple little sentence in the Code the movie audiences would be exposed to such visual details in the films as disfigured, dismembered, bloodstained and mutilated bodies, close-up views of dying men, and hair-raising details of inhuman treatment. The Code, however, under this provision bans such details from the screen, permitting their introduction into a picture only by way of indirect suggestion.

Chapter XVII

CRIME THEMES

With the analysis of the crime regulations and amendments contained in the motion picture Production Code given in the previous chapter, the reader will be better able to understand the reasons underlying their specific application to the various crime themes discussed in the subsequent pages. The themes being herein considered are those which are most frequently encountered in screen dramatization. They may form the basic theme in many cases, and, in other instances, they may be merely supplementary and incidental to the main plot. In any event, the general crime regulations and the specific examples offered should, together, afford the reader a criterion by which he may reasonably judge the treatment of any additional crime themes or subjects which may come to his mind.

The themes and subjects being considered in this chapter are:

Arson
Banditry
Bootlegging
Burglary
Counterfeiting
Drug Traffic or Smuggling
Forgery
Gambling
Gangster stories
Heroes
Kidnaping or Illegal
    Abduction

Killing in Self-defense
The "Lone Wolf"
Lynching
Murder
Perjury
Revenge Crimes
Robbery
Sabotage
Sex Crimes
Social Themes

Arson

The difficulty in dramatizing a screen story with arson as its basic plot arises because of the necessity in such a story for visual details which are forbidden by the Code. The introduction and details of the incendiary origin of the fire; the emphasis necessarily placed upon the element of frequent and extensive destruction of buildings; and the need for showing the gruesome loss of human life associated with the burning of such dwelling places, are all details forbidden by the Code provisions. The regulations require that such "details of crime" and "action showing the taking of human life" should be cut to the minimum inasmuch as "the frequent presentation of murder tends to lessen regard for the sacredness of life."

The particular danger in such a theme is its possible effect on the pyromaniac, either potential or actual, who, upon witnessing such a spectacle, might easily be definitely influenced to commit similar atrocities. Because of this danger, arson is never acceptable as a *basic* theme for the screen. Where arson occurs as an *incident* in a film drama, it should never be more than *suggested,* so that no "instructive details" may provide the basis for a complaint of "teaching methods of crime." The criminal, of course, must always be shown to be apprehended and punished for the crime. Needless to say, a pyromaniac may never be made the hero of a story.

Banditry

Banditry may sometimes be necessary for the plot. It should never, however, be made to seem heroic or glamorous. If it is introduced at all, it must be indicated that the bandit does not profit by his criminal activities, and that these unlawful actions do not bring him glory, but make him an outcast hunted by the law.

In a historical story, the absence of law-enforcing agencies may make apprehension of the bandit by the law illogical under certain circumstances. If introduced in this way, the particular need—to keep the story within the provisions of the Code—is to avoid romanticizing the bandit by making his escapades seem daring or heroic.

In stories dealing with the present day, or such periods in history when law-enforcing agencies were empowered to deal with such criminals, it must be indicated that the bandit is apprehended and punished for his crimes.

It is apparent from the foregoing that banditry alone cannot form the basic theme of the story, for then it would be necessary to emphasize the very elements forbidden by the Code. Where banditry is introduced as a supplementary element in a screen story, it may be satisfactorily treated if it is definitely established that banditry is wrong, and that it is not a solution or a justifiable means to any end, however worthy the motive may appear at the outset. The point which the Code seeks to make is that lawlessness should never be justified or be used to fight lawlessness while law is operative to function in its place. Where the law is not operative, as little as possible should be introduced relating to the activities of a bandit for the reason that under such circumstances it would not be possible to convince the audience that banditry is wrong and unlawful. On the contrary, the general impression would most likely be that banditry is a very romantic crime.

Bootlegging

If the story deals with gangsters and their bootlegging activities during the prohibition era, the theme would be subject to the regulations governing gangster stories.

That is, the story would be prohibited for picturization under the provisions forbidding the showing of gangster characters "armed and in violent conflict with the law or law-enforcing officers."

If, on the other hand, the bootlegger to be portrayed were to be a typical "moonshiner," not associated with any organized gangs, this theme might be introduced in a screen story. The chief concern for such a story under the Code would be the "details of crime," and excessive gunplay and killings. If murder occurs, it would be necessary to treat this element in accordance with the special Code provisions relating to murder; and it would also be necessary to indicate that the murderer is apprehended and punished for the crime.

Ordinarily this subject is introduced and treated as a factor incidental to the main theme, with emphasis on a love story or other acceptable concurrent plot.

Burglary

Burglary may never be made the basic theme of a story; and, where introduced as an incident, the method of breaking into a house and stealing can never be shown in detail, in accordance with the regulations prohibiting "details of crime."

Theft in itself is ordinarily considered a larceny, but inasmuch as burglary for the purpose of larceny is usually attempted with a deadly weapon and the intent to assault, it often develops into murder or rape. Crime statistics indicate that actual assault occurs in a large number of such attempts, and for this reason burglary has been classified by law as a felony.

Because of the dangers to which it exposes an entire household, this crime is of exceeding social concern, aside from the question of theft; hence the Code would never countenance a story which tends to romanticize a burglar and thus incite others to crime.

Needless to say, a burglar can never be made the hero of a screen story. Where it is necessary to the plot of the story to indicate a burglary, the burglar must always be apprehended and punished by the law for his crime. Burglary may not be introduced even as an incident, however, where not absolutely essential to the plot.

Counterfeiting

In a story dealing with counterfeiting, care must be taken not to go into detail either as to the methods employed in making money, or as to the agencies used in getting it into circulation. Since, also, United States currency may never be photographed, the writer would do well not to introduce any dramatic element requiring the photographing of money for the screen.

The counterfeiter and his criminal associates must, of course, be actually apprehended by the law, and punishment indicated for all involved in the crime.

Drug Traffic or Smuggling

The Code specifically prohibits any theme based on the drug traffic in the following provision:

"The illegal drug traffic must *never* be presented. Because of its evil consequences, the drug traffic should not be presented in any form. The existence of the trade should not be brought to the attention of audiences."

Any details of the drug traffic or of the smuggling of drugs violate the above specific Code provision, as well as the general regulations forbidding "details of crime." This means, of course, that an opium den could not be shown in pictures, and an opium fiend or other drug addict could not be made the character of a screen story.

The obvious social reason for forbidding any references to illegal drugs is the possibility that such references may suggest the place and manner in which drugs may be secured, or arouse unhealthy curiosity on the subject. All this, it is felt, tends to aggravate an already deplorable social condition, and, consequently, is not a fit subject for screen portrayal.

Occasionally a picture has appeared showing an agent of the law in pursuit of "smugglers," and the suggestion has very discreetly been made that the contents being smuggled were "drugs." In such cases, however, the drug itself was never specifically mentioned; and the main theme of the story concerned itself, not with the methods of smuggling but with the chase and the capture of the criminals. The present tendency, however, is to disallow even the use of the term "drugs" in connection with smuggling. Naturally, the methods of distributing illegal drugs, and of "peddling" dope may never be shown, since this is a part of the "traffic" in drugs.

Forgery

The methods of obtaining signatures, and the details of forging the signatures can never be made part of a plot in a screen play, as these are considered "details of crime," and, therefore, prohibited under the Code. Where forgery is required for the plot, it may, of course, be indirectly suggested, but its methods may never be shown in detail. The forger must always be apprehended by the law and punished for his crime.

Gambling

The Code regulations prohibiting "details of crime" apply with particular force to gambling. The method and manner of operating illegal and crooked gambling devices must never be shown in detail. Where it is absolutely essential to the plot to indicate that there is gambling, and crooked operation, they may be *suggested*.

Money must never be in evidence at gaming tables, card tables, or even in the ubiquitous dice games. Censor boards everywhere are averse to the portrayal of gambling and forbid the showing of money in connection with gambling.

Gambling establishments must never be associated with, or identifiable as, houses of assignation or prostitution. Particular care must be taken so that no character will give the impression that the gambling establishment is anything but a gambling place. Any suggestion of prostitution, assignation, or solicitation is strictly forbidden under the Code provision which reads:

"Brothels and houses of ill-fame, no matter of what country, are not proper locations for drama. They suggest to the average person at once sex sin, or they excite an unwholesome and morbid curiousity in the minds of youth."

Where gambling is an important element in a screen story, and much of the atmosphere and action of the picture is concerned with such a locale, care must be taken not to invest gambling with glamour, or to make it appear highly profitable. Generally speaking, where gambling gives the impression of "easy money," and so becomes an anti-social factor, compensating values must be introduced to offset this suggestion. This is in accordance with the Code principles which state that "Correct standards of life shall, as far as possible, be presented." In the words of the Production Code Administration:

"It is a reprehensible mistake, to say the least, and it is positively wrong when done beyond dramatic requirements, to tantalize youth by flaunting before it flashy clothes, *easy money,* luxurious living, habitual drinking, *gambling,* cynical contempt for conventions, and all the realism of problems that do not trouble an average person's existence."

Because of the aversion of censor boards to the subject of gambling, and the attitude of the Code toward this theme, it is best not to make the hero a gambler; or, if he is shown as a gambler, to have him relinquish gambling for some other means of livelihood.

Gangster Stories

With a view to putting an end to old and new-fashioned gangster pictures, the Board of Directors of the Motion Picture Producers & Distributors of America, Inc., ordained in September, 1935, that, for a period to be decided by the Board, the following rule would be in force, to be terminated at the discretion of the Board:

"Crime stories are not to be approved when they portray the activities of American gangsters, armed and in violent conflict with the law or law-enforcing officers."

The gangster story, or the story of organized crime, has had a place in the literary and film world only second to that of a whooping detective yarn. It has always been one of the easiest plots to devise and one of the most thrilling to see. Its popularity resulted in an unprecedented cycle of gangster films which created a public furore resulting in a sweeping change in the type of gangster film shown.

The particular objections to the old type gangster film, which includes the stories in which the G-man was the hero, were to be found in the thesis of the story, and the type of characters portrayed. The wholesale slaughter shown in these gangster films made human life appear very "cheap"; the use of weapons by the low type of humanity represented in the gangster popularized the theory that a gun could make a god out of the most "ornery" human by putting the power of death into his hands; the despotic control of the gang leader over his henchmen portrayed very graphically how unbridled evil and cunning could be used to sate the lust for power. Finally, the wealth and physical enjoyments which were the product of criminal activities had the tendency to invest crime with glamour and the charm of "easy money." Even at their death, the gangsters usually went out in a burst of glory, and, to the eyes of the youngster, at least, they died valiantly with a smoking gun in their hands.

We still have the story of organized crime with us, but in a modified form. First of all, the details of crime are forbidden. The activities of the criminals must be largely established by suggestion only. Secondly, wholesale slaughter is no longer permitted to be shown, either in warfare between groups of criminals, or between criminals and the police or other law-enforcing officers. In fact, no police officers, bank guards, private detectives, or other private or public servants of the law can be shown actually dying at the hands of criminals. Where the death of an officer results from an encounter with criminals, it can be indirectly suggested. Third, the tough type of individual formerly used to portray a gangster is no longer allowed for screen presentation. This means that the hard-looking, foul-speaking type, eager to kill, is banned from screen stories. He has been replaced with a new type of criminal suggestive of a racketeer rather than a "gangster." Instead of being hard-looking, he appears to be a gentleman with at least a surface polish. Instead of using foul speech, he is soft-spoken and businesslike in his conversation rather than "tough." Finally, instead of showing an eagerness to kill, he is eager to avoid killing, preferring to use his wits to gain his ends rather than to use weapons, to resort to scheming rather than to violence. The danger of building up the racketeer as a central character, dominating his group, is avoided by making him more or less anonymous—as one of a group of associates who operate as partners.

It is easy to see that the "racketeer" type is not readily imitated, nor do his exploits seem glamorous. Even the romantic touch has been removed from such stories by the rigid regulations dealing with sex which prohibit either showing or suggesting any illicit sex relationship between the criminal and his female associates. If the love interest is introduced at all, it can have no connotation of illicit sex about it. It is obvious that in a crime story of this type it would be practically impossible to introduce the necessary compensating moral values required by the Code for the treatment of illicit sex. This automatically bars from these stories the luxurious, sensual atmosphere generally associated with gangster themes.

According to the dictates of the Code requiring that the law be triumphant at all times, it is necessary, of course, to indicate that the racketeers are apprehended by the law and punished for their crimes.

·   ·   ·

In London, the British Board of Censors has made some interesting observations regarding the reception of the "gangster" film in the British Empire, which appear to sustain the wisdom of the Board of Directors of the Producers' Association in their curtailment of this type of film. The Board says:

"Closely allied to the 'Horror' film is the 'Gangster' film. There is a new type of film being introduced here from America, or, may I say, an old type in a new garment, namely, a revival of the 'gangster' film which purports to show the determination of the Federal Government to stamp out gangster activities. In these recent productions, the hero is the policeman, and not the criminal. In the old films, which gave us so much trouble a few years ago, I admit the gangsters generally came to a sticky end. If the contrary had been the case, and crime had been glorified, these films would not have been certificated by us. In the new variation the whole of the gangster's gamut of crime, murder, kidnaping, robbery with violence, arson, etc., are just as prominently portrayed as of yore. I consider that the cumulative effect of this type of film is highly undesirable. I discussed this point with the representatives of the American 'Production Code' committee during their recent visit to London, and found that they were fully alive to, and in general agreement with our views. They explained that the subject of these films had been very carefully and fully discussed at Hollywood prior to production, but permission had been granted to make a limited number from this new angle, namely, Government activity in fighting crime. I trust that we shall not have a recrudescence of these subjects, for I believe, as I have already said, that their influence is unwholesome."

Heroes

The Code specifically states that "Criminals should not be made heroes, even if they are *historical* criminals." This regulation provokes the question, "When is a character definitely a criminal?" The infraction of the law by an individual, though punishable by imprisonment, does not always characterize the individual as a "criminal" within the concept of the Code. It is the habitual criminal rather than the first offender who comes under this classification.

The weaknesses in human nature which make man give way to temptation, and the strength of character which brings about his reform and regeneration have always been, and will always be among the most powerful elements in poignant drama. Therefore it is not the intention of the Code to bar these portrayals from the screen. On the contrary, there is no objection to such a characterization in film drama. Many pictures have been made showing the regeneration of an offender, and both men and women have been shown to turn from criminal pursuits to honorable employment.

If the hero or heroine is shown to commit a crime, he or she must also be shown to repent of such wrongdoing and to make restitution for any loss for which he or she may be responsible, thru theft, cheating, etc. Whether or not there is to be punishment depends, of course, upon the magnitude of the offense. The law should be shown to take a logical course. If consistent with the practice of law, pardon or probation of the offender may be suggested, in some cases. Even a paroled convict may be a hero if the story concerns itself with his regeneration.

The Code, however, definitely bans certain types of criminals for presentation on the screen as heroes. Thus a gangster cannot be made a hero; nor can a racketeer who is the prototype of the gangster; the kidnaper; the hardened and unregenerate type of criminal; or the type of character who seeks to fight crime by using criminal methods and so romanticizes crime and makes it appear heroic and praiseworthy.

A hero or heroine who plans to commit a crime, but does not go thru with it because of moral scruples may be dramatized as a sympathetic character—provided that the story throws its emphasis upon the moral ethics which turn the principal character from the commission of the crime, and not upon the crime itself. The story would then become a story of regeneration rather than one of crime.

If the hero is to be characterized as an offender against the law, the story must indicate a complete regeneration. Temporary reform would not be sufficient. There must be a complete reversal of the principal's viewpoint. In the words of the Production Code Administration, the offender must be shown to suffer sufficiently from his crime "to turn from it with loathing." The lesson that crime does not pay must be a thoro one; and the reform and regeneration must be complete. Unless these requirements are met, the offender, or criminal, may never be made the hero of a screen story.

Kidnaping or Illegal Abduction

The wave of child kidnaping which swept the United States after the Lindbergh case was reflected in the frequent depiction of kidnaping on the screen, until the law-enforcement agencies demanded that an end be put to such suggestions thru a medium with as powerful an appeal to the imagination and as widespread an influence as the motion pictures. The Producers' Association offered its cooperation to government agencies and, consequently, the kidnaping regulations, outlined in the crime amendments, came into being. They specifically forbade showing, or even *suggesting,* the kidnaping of a child. Further, the details of kidnaping were banned from the screen, even where an adult was the victim. These Code regulations specifically outlined in the section titled "Re Crime in Motion Pictures" read as follows:

1. Kidnaping may *not* be the main theme of the story.
2. The person kidnaped *may not be a child.*
3. No "details of the crime of kidnaping" may be shown.
4. No profit may accrue to the abductors or kidnapers.
5. *The kidnapers must be punished.*

This does not mean, of course, that kidnaping may never be suggested in a screen story. Kidnaping may be introduced as an incidental part of the plot. However, the actual abduction may not be shown in detail. It may only be suggested. The object in this restriction is to avoid suggesting the methods or manner in which kidnaping may be executed.

The kidnap victim may *never* be a child, irrespective of the manner of plot treatment. This means that even the suggestion in a story that a child has been kidnaped is *unacceptable* under the Code. The kidnaped person must always be an adult. There is no exception to this rule.

Kidnaping, even as an incidental part of the plot, may never be introduced without the compensating values outlined above. It must be definitely established that the kidnapers do not profit by the kidnaping; and they must be apprehended and punished for the crime.

In restricting the theme of kidnaping to an incidental element in a screen story, the Code practically puts an end to the old-fashioned kidnaping pictures such as the one titled "Miss Fane's Baby is Stolen." This type of kidnaping picture concerned itself wholly with the abduction, the writing and delivery of ransom notes, the intimidation of the kidnap victim and his family and the detailed activities of the kidnapers, in avoiding detection. Under the present Code provisions most of these details would have to be omitted; and the main theme of the story would have to concern itself with some subject other than that of kidnaping.

Killing in Self-Defense

It is entirely acceptable under the Code to introduce a killing in self-defense into a screen story. However, even where the killing is thus justified, the law must be shown to take its proper course. The guilty party must be taken into legal custody or offer himself voluntarily to the police, for the law alone has the power and the right to exonerate him. A story should never suggest that a killing in self-defense can be successfully kept secret, or that it may be excused on its own merits either by the guilty party or his intimates. It is not necessary to dramatize in detail the apprehension and trial of the guilty party in such an instance—it is sufficient to indicate in a few lines of dialog that the guilty party will have no difficulty in proving his innocence on the plea of self-defense.

The "Lone Wolf"

Under this heading would come the jewel thief operating by himself; a swindler, or "confidence" man, or other type of offender who may be engaged in shady dealings which place him outside the pale of legitimate business. A story dealing with this type may be acceptably treated for the screen for the reason that such a character depends upon his wits rather than upon weapons in his illegal exploits. The Code provisions regarding the treatment of crime, and the prohibitions relating to "details of crime" would apply in testing the acceptability of these stories. The offender must be apprehended by the law and punished for any illegal acts he may commit. If he repents of his conduct, relinquishes his criminal activities and seeks to make restitution for any wrong he has done, it is possible to indicate that he is placed on probation. The law itself, however, would have to exonerate him and to free him from the necessity of punishment.

Lynching

Lynching is sometimes a necessary incident in a screen story. Where it is introduced, the minimum of detail must be given, particularly in the formation and rioting of a lynching mob.

The lynching itself may never be more than suggested. When it is essential to the story to show a lynching, it must be established that it is wrong to attempt to curb lawlessness thru means of lawlessness. Of course, where lynching occurs in a drama dealing with a period in history in which no law was operative, the lynching would not in itself be unlawful; but care would need to be taken with the gruesome details as indicated above. Censor boards frown upon this element in screen stories; hence it should never be introduced unless it is absolutely needed for proper plot motivation.

Murder

A murder, whether committed by a character in a mystery story or in any other plot, is subject specifically to the provisions of the Code prohibiting the details of crime.

To meet the requirements of the Code prohibiting "details of crime," a murder story must be dramatized in such a way that it does not emphasize the *details* relative to the *planning* and *execution* of the murder, and, further, that it does not contain any great amount of *detailed discussion* concerning the method of committing the murder. While, of course, it is the object of a mystery story to show how the murder has been committed, this can be done without divulging each step taken by the murderer in the planning and execution of his crime. The object of forbidding these details is to make certain that the screen play will not serve as a medium to teach methods of crime. Many of these can be merely *suggested*.

To meet the further requirement that "action showing the taking of human life, *even in the mystery stories*, is to be cut to the minimum" because "these frequent presentations of murder tend to lessen regard for the sacredness of life," the writer should be scrupulously careful not to introduce any murder unless it is absolutely essential to plot motivation. This is particularly important in stories where a number of murders occur. Those which can be omitted without spoiling the story should be deleted. No murder may be introduced merely to provide "punch" in a story.

In addition to the above regulations, the following provisions must also be fully met before a story can be considered acceptable for screen presentation:

1. Murder must be definitely and affirmatively characterized as wrong;
2. Murder must never be condoned;
3. Murder must never be made to appear "right and acceptable" under any circumustances;
4. Audience sympathy must not be created for the crime;
5. The murderer must be *punished* by due process of law. (He should not escape punishment by suicide.)

Murder stories may generally be classified as:

1. Those in which the murderer is the villain of the story;
2. Those in which the hero, or another sympathetic character commits a murder ostensibly for a worthy or excusable purpose.

Little difficulty is presented by the first class of murder story, for the audience instinctively condemns the murderer and the crime. The second class, however, requires particular care in treatment to avoid a justification of murder. All stories in the second class should

be carefully analyzed under the provisions given above
in order to provide the compensating moral values
demanded by the Code.

The first provision requires that murder be characterized as wrong—as lawless and criminal, and so grave an
offense that it is never justified. It cannot be right to
kill, no matter how great the provocation. Society would
be thrown into a chaotic state if the theory were to be
generally accepted that there are times when one is justified in murdering another if the net result is a good one
and in the interests of society. Personal prejudices,
rather than justice, would be served by such a belief.
Therefore, murder is never to be justified whether it is
committed by the hero or the villain.

This point is very important. If the hero or sympathetic character in a story is shown to commit murder as
a means of retribution or to serve some other apparently
justifiable end, the audience is likely to forget that
murder, *per se,* is wrong, and to feel that it may be
right some times. Such a reaction is definitely dangerous
and anti-social, and for this reason any story which seeks
to justify murder is automatically disqualified for screen
presentation.

Where there is danger of giving the impression that
murder is excusable, the murder should be condemned as
wrong, and an affirmative stand should be taken in behalf
of lawful action to meet the particular issue or problem.
This latter is not only a strong moral element, but a
forceful dramatic element as well. It must be established that it is wrong to use lawlessness to fight lawlessness, and that a lawful solution is the only right solution.
The attitude should be that "two wrongs do not make a
right." The hero, if he be the murderer, should be
shown to repent of his crime and to acknowledge that
his action has been inexcusable and wrong.

The second provision is important in that it denies sympathy for the murder. If the murderer finds that no one—not even those who are nearest and dearest to him—will condone or excuse the murder, and that everyone believes it to be a grave wrong that is to be severely condemned, he—and thru him, the audience—will be made to realize that murder is never justifiable.

The third and fourth provisions will be fulfilled if the foregoing points are established and if it is further made evident that, regardless of the motive which prompted it, instead of being a solution, murder only complicates the issue for everyone concerned. With emphasis on the shame, stigma and suffering which the crime brings with it to both the guilty and the innocent, there will be little danger of audience sympathy being created for the murder. Such treatment is in accordance with the provisions of the Code which read:

"Sympathy with a person who sins is not the same as sympathy with the sin or crime of which he is guilty. We may feel sorry for the plight of the murderer or even understand the circumstances which led him to his crime. We may *not* feel sympathy with the wrong which he has done."

The fifth provision is self-explanatory. It specifically forbids the escape or pardon of the murderer. It is, therefore, necessary to show that the murderer is actually apprehended—or gives himself up—and is to be punished for his crime. The murderer may not escape punishment thru suicide. The Code discourages the introduction of suicide as a means of escape from punishment, except in cases where the crime has been committed by an insane person. The plea of insanity in itself, however, unless based upon evidence previously established in the story, may never be used as a pretext to avoid punishment for murder.

As in some other themes, the element of time enters into a judgment as to the acceptability of certain phases of a murder story. If the story deals with the present day, it must be treated with the strictest regard for law and law-enforcement in accordance with the provisions given above. If, on the other hand, the story deals with a period in history when the taking of human life was more or less common and there were no stringent laws to govern such crimes, then the treatment would be allowed a wider latitude. This is particularly true in connection with the situations covered by the following Code regulation:

"In lands and ages of less developed civilization and moral principles, revenge may sometimes be presented. This would be the case especially in places where no law exists to cover the crime, because of which revenge is committed."

However, even in stories which deal with a lawless period of history, murder must be shown definitely to be wrong and productive of suffering and unhappiness. The murderer must be punished for the wrong *thru whatever medium was representative of law and order* in the period in which the crime was committed.

Perjury

Perjured testimony in a screen story must be clearly marked as wrong, as both a legal and a moral violation. It must not be condoned for any reason, however sentimental, because it cannot be "right and acceptable" to obstruct the process of law and justice by means of perjury—or to suggest that justice might be more readily assured by such wrongful means.

Where perjury is committed, it must be punished. Never must there be any suggestion that perjured testimony can be given with impunity.

Crimes Committed for Purposes of Revenge

The Code specifically states that:

"Revenge in *modern* times shall not be justified."

There is no exception to this ruling in regard to stories dealing with the *present* day. However, inasmuch as the element of time is an important factor in judging such themes, the Code goes on to make the following provisions:

"In lands and ages of less developed civilization and moral principles, revenge *may sometimes* be presented. This would be the case especially in places where no law exists to cover the crime because of which revenge is committed."

In a story dealing with modern times, the hero who seeks to take the law in his own hands to avenge a wrong, must be apprehended and punished for the crime he has committed exactly as any other criminal, or law-breaker.

The punishment to be meted out would, of course, depend upon the magnitude of the crime. The important point is to establish the fact that revenge is not justified, that it is wrong, and that punishment is inevitable and inescapable. Redress for wrongs should be sought by legal means.

An effective dramatic device in a story where the hero is seeking to avenge a wrong is to have him join some law-enforcing agency and, thus legally sanctioned and equipped, go out to "get his man" as a representative of the Law.

In regard to historical tales, the Code provisions stated above allow the treatment of such stories a wider latitude. However, in such cases it is necessary to establish that revenge is *wrong* in itself, and that lawlessness is productive of suffering and unhappiness. In the phrase "some times" the Code restricts the stories which fall within this category to those which allow some compensating moral values to be introduced to counteract the lawlessness which is portrayed. Consequently, a story must indicate punishment in some form for lawlessness in order to be acceptable under the Code. Even in lawless times the Law was represented by some individual in authority, and it is dramatically possible, therefore, to indicate punishment for lawlessness as coming thru such a medium, thus giving it authoritative legal sanction.

Robbery

Under the regulations prohibiting the "details of crime" in motion pictures, a robbery may be suggested, but may never be shown *in detail*. The most satisfactory method of indicating robbery is by *suggestion,* or indirect reference.

Excessive gunplay and flaunting of guns are also prohibited under the regulations governing "Crime in motion pictures" which specify that:

"There must be no display, at any time, of machine guns, sub-machine guns or other weapons generally classified as illegal weapons, in the hands of gangsters or other criminals," and

"The flaunting of weapons by gangsters, or other criminals, will not be allowed."

In view of the Code ruling prohibiting gangster characters and gangster warfare, the types who are to portray the robbers should not be of the hard-boiled, tough-looking gangster type. They must, of course, be apprehended and punished.

Sabotage

Sabotage is a crime most often suggested in stories dealing with mob violence. Particular care must be taken in showing such mob violence. It is questionable from the standpoint of industry policy to introduce scenes glorifying a mob and showing the wrecking of property. Therefore very little actual sabotage should be shown at any time. Where it is necessary to suggest sabotage, indirect references to the incident are the most satisfactory method of indicating that it has taken place. The visual details are prohibited by the Code as "details of crime."

Sex Crimes

Needless to say, a motion picture story may never treat of sex crimes other than rape (see Miscellaneous Sex Subjects) either by inference or suggestion, or with any torture or mutilation resulting from such crimes.

Social Themes

Sociological dramas, dealing with mob violence, social conflict, and industrial strife must conform with the following provisions of the Code:

1. The hero must not be a criminal;
2. Law and order must triumph. There must be no sympathy aroused for anti-social activities;
3. There must be no reckless destruction of property;
4. There must be no unnecessary killing;
5. Brutality must be reduced to a dramatic minimum.

To conform to the first provision, while the hero could not be a criminal, he might be a misguided person. That is, none of his acts should be of a criminal nature, and his intent and aim should not be criminal.

Whatever elements of brutality, killing, or destruction of property are introduced in such stories should be definitely limited to the requirements of proper plot motivation, and should be suggested wherever possible, rather than shown in too great detail.

These stories present so many problems from the standpoint of the Code, of general industry policy, and of censorship that no particular treatment for specific social themes can be outlined in advance. Generally speaking, however, the provisions listed above comprise the test to which all social problem themes will be subjected under the motion picture Production Code, and the story should, therefore, be written to conform to these provisions, as well as the various Code regulations pertaining to "crime in motion pictures."

SEX IN PICTURES

CHAPTER XVIII

THE SEX REGULATIONS

Year after year, stories—and many times completed pictures of both domestic and foreign production—have to be rejected because of their improper sex treatment. Among the subjects and themes continually found violating the Production Code principles, to name them in the order of their frequency, are adultery, loose sex, infidelity, and illegitimacy; prostitution, rape and seduction; and comedies based on procreation and childbirth. To mention but a few of the most objectionable elements appearing in stories, and those forbidden by the Code, may be added perversion; miscegenation; sadism; incest; impotency; the sale of women; the details of harem life; and white slavery. Stories or pictures having these subjects for their main themes can rarely be changed without completely rewriting the plot, and this one fact probably accounts more than any other for their frequent rejection by the studios.

Social problem stories, among which may be numbered themes dealing with illicit sex, divorce, adultery, and similar subjects, make up a large percentage of the pictures produced in any one year. The reiteration of these topics is bound to have a marked influence upon audiences. Just as the wrong type of crime film has been aptly termed a "school of crime," so the wrong type of film dealing with sex problems can, with equal force, be branded as a "school of immorality." It was with this social responsibility in mind that the framers of the Code propounded numerous regulations to prevent the dramatization of unsuitable subjects and to assure the moral treatment of those subjects which form the basis of legitimate story material for motion pictures.

The general principles of the Code applying to sex themes are as follows:

"1. No picture should lower the moral standards of those who see it. This is done:

    (a) When evil is made to appear *attractive,* and *good* is made to appear unattractive.

    (b) When the *sympathy* of the audience is thrown on the side of crime, wrong-doing, evil, sin. The same thing is true of a film that would throw sympathy against goodness, honor, innocence, purity, honesty.

NOTE: *Sympathy with a person who sins* is not the same as sympathy with the sin or crime of which he is guilty. We may feel sorry for the plight of the murderer or even understand the circumstances which led him to his crime; but *we may not feel sympathy with the wrong* which he has done.

2. The presentation of evil is often essential for art or fiction or drama. This in itself is not wrong, provided:

    (a) That evil is not *presented alluringly.* Even if later on the evil is condemned or punished, it must not be allowed to appear so attractive that the emotions are drawn to desire or approve so strongly that later they forget the condemnation and remember only the apparent joy of the sin.

    (b) That thruout the presentation, *evil and good are never confused* and that evil is always recognized clearly as evil.

    (c) That in the end the audience feels that evil is wrong and good is right.

3. Comedies and farces *should not make fun* of good, innocence, morality or justice."

Because certain themes require special amplified treatment under the Code, they are treated in separate chapters. These are (1) Adultery; (2) Divorce; (3) Prostitution; (4) Seduction; and (5) The Triangle involving married persons.

The subjects and themes which form but an incidental part of screen stories, or are less frequently encountered, are grouped together under the following headings:

Illicit Sex

1. The Don Juan
2. Ex-wife as Mistress
3. The Gigolo
4. Illegitimacy
5. The Mistress-Lover, or Kept Woman
6. The Transitory or Single Affair by Mutual **Consent**

Marriage

1. Bigamy
2. Companionate or Trial Marriage
3. Birth Control
4. Honeymoon or First Night Scenes
5. Impotency
6. Marital Relations
7. Polygamy
8. Procreation

Miscellaneous Sex Subjects

1. Abortion
2. Childbirth
3. The Double Standard
4. Harems
5. Incest
6. Miscegenation
7. Pregnancy
8. Rape
9. Sale of Women
10. Sex Perversion
11. White Slavery

The provisions referred to as "Compensating moral values" in the analysis of the various sex themes, embody the general and the specific regulations of the Production Code appearing in the sections titled "Working Principles," and the "Principles of Plot," as well as the additional individual provisions which the Production Code Administration has found it necessary to add in order to insure the enforcement of both the spirit and the letter of the Code in the treatment of these themes.

CHAPTER XIX

ADULTERY

Adultery appears to be one of the most popular screen themes, if one is to take as a criterion the number of stories submitted by the studios to the Production Code Administration each year dealing with this subject. Yet four out of every five of such stories usually have to be rejected because of the fact that adultery is justified or made to appear glamorous, in violation of the Code principles.

The Production Code says, concerning adultery: "Adultery as a subject should be avoided." The Production Code Administration discourages the use of this theme for motion pictures because it is extremely difficult to create a screen story, based on adultery, in such a way as to bring out the compensating moral values demanded by the Code.

Under the section titled "Plot Material," the Code states:

"1. Adultery is *never* a fit subject for *comedy*. Thru comedy of this sort, ridicule is thrown on the essential relationships of home and family and marriage, and illicit relationships are made to seem permissible, and either delightful or daring.

2. Sometimes adultery must be counted on as material occurring in *serious drama*. In this case (a) it should not appear to be justified; (b) it should not be used to weaken respect for marriage; and (c) it should not be presented as attractive or alluring."

The following *compensating moral values* are used by the Production Code Administration to test the acceptability of a story based on adultery:

I.   Adultery must never appear to be justified.

II. The sinful relationship must not be condoned— that is, there must not be general indifference to it, nor tacit or express acceptance or approval of it.

III. No dialog or action should indicate any disrespect of marriage beyond the necessary portrayal of the sin.

IV. Divorce should not be shown to take place except for sound reasons, and as a last resort.

V.   Bedroom scenes should be avoided; and physical contact between the principals should be reduced to the absolute minimum.

VI. Adultery must not be presented as attractive and alluring—there must be no more glamour and luxury than is consonant with the plot.

VII. Regeneration or retribution should be satisfactory to compensate for the wrong.

I. Adultery Must Never be Justified

Adultery, representing as it does, a gross violation of the marriage pact, always requires some explanation for its occurrence. The motive, in novels at least, has found justification under numerous plausible guises. The provocation, according to time-honored dramatic devices, is ordinarily attributable to the rebellion of a husband or a wife against the indifference, the neglect, the coldness, and, even, the cruelty, of the spouse. The invalidism or insanity of the marriage partner in themselves constitute not unusual, though somewhat melodramatic, motives for the commission of adultery. The bewitchery, charm and blandishments of the third party, too, are recounted as potent factors in enchanting the reason of the intractable spouse.

In a screen story there is no objection to starting out with any one of these marital and domestic conditions. But when a story, starting from any of these premises, seeks to *justify adultery* as an expedient, as revenge, or merely as a relief from the cares and responsibilities imposed by matrimony, then the story violates the Code provision requiring that "Adultery must never be justified."

In the eyes of the Code, granting that the provocative conditions exist creative of matrimonial disharmony, to justify adultery for these or any other reasons would obviously, to quote the regulations, "throw the sympathy of the audience on the side of wrong-doing and evil." The views of the Production Code Administration, in interpreting the Code on this issue, are expressed in unmistakable terms in its statement that, "No good reason can be given for adultery; it can not be right; and the audience must not be persuaded or deceived into thinking that good reason and sufficient cause do exist for the transgression, and that it is right."

For the purpose of this discussion the term "adulterous mate" will be used to refer to the husband or wife who commits the adultery, and the term "innocent mate" will indicate the other partner to the marriage.

To avoid a justification of the adultery, the adulterous mate should not be shown in too sympathetic a light; and, contrariwise, the innocent mate should not be made to appear too unsympathetic a character. If audience sympathy is too strongly aroused for the transgressor, the spectator would unconsciously tend to condone the subsequent adultery. If the character delineation of the wife and husband is carefully drawn with this factor in mind, the audience will not be drawn to sympathize with the wrong-doer.

The third party, naturally, cannot be portrayed in an attractive fashion. He or she is, potentially, the villain— the party who seeks to break up the marriage, the home and the family. The audience must not sympathize with him or with her.

II. *Adultery must not be condoned*

The intent of the Code in this provision is quite clearly expressed in its amplification of the regulation— "there must not be general indifference to it, nor tacit or express acceptance or approval of it." This means that no character in the story should condone the wrong.

These precautions are not as far-fetched as they would appear to be on the surface. It is not at all unusual in stories of this kind to find the wife condoning the adultery of the husband. This attitude is accepted, in the minds of writers at least, as part of the "politics" of marriage. But the Code looks upon the defections even of a husband with grave concern. It recognizes no "double standard" of conduct. Consequently, where adultery is introduced into the plot the wife must not, and can not, be shown to remain indifferent to it—to tacitly condone the action by pretending to be unaware of it—or to ignore it in the hope that the affair will come to an end. She must condemn the wrong, and make her husband realize the seriousness of what he has done or is doing.

III. *No dialog or action should indicate disrespect of marriage*

Any dialog on the part of any character in the story which would belittle marriage as an institution is naturally undesirable in a picture dealing with adultery. Any flippant remarks about marriage would be equally objectionable under this provision of the Code. A serious attitude toward the responsibilities and vows of marriage should always be manifest in motion pictures. The portrayal of the sin in itself, of course, is necessary to establish the fact that adultery has been committed. Beyond the meagre details necessary to make the illicit relationship obvious, there should be as little insinuation as possible that the extra-marital relationship possesses a charm exceeding that of a happy marriage. It were better, under the Code provisions at least, that the contrary impression be given. This is not difficult when it is considered that the violation of civil, social, and moral law necessarily brings with it a chaotic emotional state which does not permit the offenders to take their joys with any sense of ease. The quirks of conscience, the uncertainty of the duration of such a relationship, and the questionable morality of the characters involved more than suggest the unpleasant phases of the illicit affair.

IV. Divorce should not take place except for sound reasons, and as a last resort

The Code, in insisting that a more serious attitude be taken toward the responsibilities of marriage, is but expressing the trend of the times. With this thought in mind, the correct treatment of divorce in a story dealing with adultery suggests itself.

V. Bedroom scenes should be avoided

Scenes of intimacy, particularly those which are intended to imply passion, should be restricted not only in their ardour, but also as concerns their locale. Bedrooms are bad dramatic locations in stories dealing with illicit relationships. The Code considers passion as an unfit subject for screen presentation under any circumstances.

VI.   *Adultery must not be presented as attractive*

In saying that "there must be no more glamour and luxury than is consonant with the plot," the Production Code Administration intends to say that if the wife, for instance, is married to a husband making an average salary and they live in an average home, her adulterous affair with another man should not suddenly transport her into a world of luxury such as she has never known before. Of course, if the story is concerned with the peregrinations of the wealthy, then the fairy story atmosphere would not be introduced with the origin of the illicit affair, since the atmosphere would be consistent thruout and luxury would be "consonant with the plot." The idea of a "Cinderella" transformation, however, thru the *modus operandi* of immorality is hardly a presentable thought to give the impressionable part of an audience to toy with.

VII.   *Regeneration or Retribution*

The compensating moral values require that regeneration *or* retribution should be satisfactory to compensate for the wrong.

Regeneration is usually preceded by repentance. The Code requires that whenever the regeneration of a character is indicated, it must be shown that the wrong-doer has suffered sufficiently from the wrong-doing *to learn a lesson from it.* That is one sure way to take the glamour out of sinning. After the adulterous mate, therefore, has made himself or herself thoroly miserable by his or her inexcusable conduct, repentance is a natural by-product. Regeneration has really taken place when the wrong-doer earnestly and sincerely strives to do the right thing because he knows that he will be happier that way. And the audience, after sitting thru several harrowing reels showing the transgressor's suffering, thinks so, too. And since the audience reaction is the most important objective of the film, the moral requirements are fully met.

On the other hand, if the transgressor does not repent, in spite of suffering, then he or she is a hardened and deliberate wrong-doer and must be shown to come to a tragic end, according to the Code provisions. The tragedy provides the "retribution."

The "third party," whoever he or she may be, must be shown to suffer some loss because of the part which this party has played in the tragic affair. He cannot escape unscathed. After all, he or she is, in essence, the "villain."

CHAPTER XX

DIVORCE

The Production Code requirement that marriage be treated as an enduring obligation and divorce as a serious matter, reflects the current trend of thought. The subject of divorce, though not mentioned directly in the Production Code, comes within its provisions which seek to protect the institution of marriage. For instance, the Code specifically states that, "The sanctity of the institution of marriage and the home shall be upheld"; and also that, "The treatment should not throw sympathy against marriage as an institution."

The following points should be kept in mind when analyzing a screen story:

(1) Divorce, allowed by the law of the land, should be shown to take place only for sound reasons and as a last resort.

(2) Divorce should not be lightly resorted to as the solution of matrimonial problems.

(3) No dialog or action should be disrespectful of marriage.

Divorce by Collusion

If it is necessary to indicate a divorce in a screen story, it should not be shown that it is obtained by means of collusion, since this is an illegal and immoral method of securing a divorce.

Multiple Divorces

There is no objection to indicating that the principal in the story has been divorced more than once; but care should be taken not to suggest that divorces can be obtained primarily for the purpose of collecting alimony and living a free and easy life. Of course, a story showing one divorce after another undertaken casually and flippantly could not be transferred to the screen.

Annulment of Marriage

Annulment of marriage in itself offers no problem, except that of whether or not the reasons for which annulment is sought are of a nature that can be discussed, under the Code.

CHAPTER XXI

ILLICIT SEX

Perhaps more than any other single theme, the story dealing with illicit sex is the most difficult to treat for the screen. To the ordinary reader this will seem strange; but those who have ever glimpsed the average Hollywood writer's idea of a story based on this subject will understand whence the difficulty arises. For it is not so much the stringent rules of the Production Code that complicate the problem, but, alas, the product itself. It seems that too many writers work on the principle that they can't woo their muse anywhere but in the gutter. Consequently, when these stories come under the test of the Code, they either must be rejected outright, or the flaming inspiration of the screen writer must be clipped into the wastebasket by reams.

If screen writers were required to take an apprenticeship in public taste by writing for the popular national magazines, they would most probably purge themselves of the libidinous touch. Contrary to the popular delusion, the public does not like the facts of life fed to them in the "raw." If anyone is inclined to doubt this, all he has to do is to try and sell such a story. One of the first and foremost rules of popular magazine writing is to avoid any suggestion of salaciousness.

The Production Code has gone into great detail in regard to its prohibitions on the subject of illicit sex. Specifically, under "Plot Material," the Code states that, "Sexual immorality is sometimes necessary for the plot."

It then goes on to explain and to itemize the general principles for the treatment of plots dealing with sex, passion and incidents relating to them, as follows:

"All legislators have recognized clearly that there are in normal human beings emotions which react naturally and spontaneously to the presentation of certain definite manifestations of sex and passion.

"The presentation of scenes, episodes, plots, etc., which are deliberately meant to excite these manifestations on the part of the audience is always wrong, is subversive of the interest of society, and a peril to the human race.

"Sex and passion exist and consequently must sometimes enter into the stories which deal with human beings."

The Code goes on to say that:

"*Impure love,* the love of man and woman forbidden by human and divine law, must be presented in such a way that:
1. It is clearly known by the audience to be wrong;
2. Its presentation does not excite sexual reactions, mental or physical, in an ordinary audience;
3. It must not be presented as attractive and beautiful;
4. It must not be the subject of comedy or farce, or treated as the material for laughter;
5. It must not be presented in such a way as to arouse passion or *morbid curiosity* on the part of the audience;
6. It must not be made to seem right and permissible;
7. In general, it *must not be detailed in method or manner.* Excessive and lustful kissing, lustful embraces, suggestive postures and gestures are not to be shown."

The Code also states that while *scenes of passion* are sometimes necessary for the plot, they are subject to the following restrictions:

"a. They should appear only where necessary and not as an added stimulus to the emotions of the audience.
b. When not essential to the plot, they should not occur.
c. They must not be explicit in action, nor vivid in method, e.g., by handling of the body, by lustful and prolonged kissing, by evidently lustful embraces, by positions which strongly arouse passions."

The Code adds a final warning on this subject under the heading of "Locations," in the statement:

"Bedrooms: In themselves they are perfectly innocent. Their suggestion may be kept innocent. However, under certain conditions they are bad dramatic locations.

Their use in a comedy or farce (on the principle of the so-called bedroom farce) is wrong, because they suggest sex laxity and obscenity."

With these principles in mind, the dramatic treatment of the themes appearing in the subsequent pages is more or less evident. Others, as indicated, are prohibited for screen dramatization altogether.

The Don Juan

The "Don Juan" is a character beloved of fiction because of the romantic cloak over his immoralities. This theme is an unfit subject for screen treatment because such a character makes "evil appear attractive." The irresponsible and immoral philosophy represented by this traditional character tends to "teach youth false values of life," and thru his flippant disregard of moral standards "tends to lower the moral standards" of those who witness such a portrayal. This refers, of course, to the died-in-the-wool type of Don Juan who spends his nocturnal hours leaping over balconies.

The hero of a screen story may not be made an immoral character without the introduction of compensating moral values to offset such a portrayal. To write a screen story about a charming, romantic young chap is perfectly acceptable. He may have mercurial affections and lose his heart anew with every turn of the weathervane; but if he breaks the moral law, he must be shown to pay the penalty in some form of suffering. As the picturization of a light-hearted young gentleman seems to have

in it no place for tragedy and suffering, the solution is
to characterize him as a decent young fellow.

Ex-Wife as Mistress

An ex-wife may not be shown in a screenplay to
become the mistress of her former husband, since such
an action would be immoral and the relationship an
illicit one exactly as if they had never been married.
It would be quite difficult to introduce any "compensating moral values" for such action which would be at all
convincing to audiences.

Gigolo

The gigolo, or male counterpart of the "mistress" or
"kept woman," cannot be portrayed on the screen. Even
the word "gigolo" may not be employed, as all censor
boards, both here and abroad, delete it.

Illegitimacy

Illegitimacy is always concurrent with a plot of illicit
sex, adultery, or seduction, and is subject to the regulations and provisions governing these specific themes.

This theme is a very questionable one and should
be introduced only when it is absolutely necessary for
the development of the plot. No direct or crude references should be made to the illegitimacy, and it must
never be discussed in detail. Once the child's illegitimacy
has been established, the fact should be left out of the
discussion. Undue emphasis upon this fact is likely to
arouse morbid curiousity on the part of the youthful
members of the audience.

Often in such a theme it is found necessary to indicate the ill-treatment of the child. If so, the ill-treatment
should not be justified—it should be definitely indicated

that an innocent child should not be made to suffer for its parents' sin.

Mistress-Lover, or "Kept Woman"

The illicit relationship maintained for a period of time which comes under this classification is generally considered to be "habitual unlawful cohabitation." If one of the parties to such an affair is married, the story must be treated in accordance with the specific Code regulations given in the chapter titled *adultery*.

This type of story, dealing with unmarried persons, is very difficult to treat for the screen, not only because it requires for its dramatization many details prohibited by the Code, but also because such relationships are looked upon with tolerance by many people with the result that justification of immorality and sympathy for wrong-doing is inherent in the theme.

The screen mood of any story based on this theme is necessarily an unhappy one, and, often, a tragic one, since the Code demands that the relationship be shown not only to be wrong, but to be productive of suffering and punishment.

The Code prohibits the details of illicit sex. The pair could not be actually shown living together; nor could such cohabitation even be suggested. Where it is possible to write a story dealing with this theme which does not give the sensuous details of the affair, and which, at the same time, does not justify or glorify the affair but definitely establishes the fact that it is morally wrong and productive of unhappy consequences, it may be made into a screenplay. But not otherwise.

The Transitory or Single Affair by Mutual Consent

This type of affair is considered as an illicit sex relationship between unmarried persons (if a married person is involved, it is adultery and subject to the treatment outlined for such a theme), in which the woman voluntarily surrenders. It may not be introduced as an incident in a screen story unless absolutely essential for plot motivation. Where it is required for the development of the plot, such an affair may be suggested only when the proper compensating moral values are emphasized. This provision has had to be enforced because of the tendency of stories to add "punch" by having several illicit affairs going on between lesser characters in the story, as well as the "grand passion" of the principals.

It is, of course, much easier to treat a transitory affair than it is to handle the mistress theme, because in the former the sex affair is not the main theme of the story. Particular care is necessary that the affair be not openly and explicitly established by detailed dialog indicating the origin and progress of the liaison, or by action emphasizing the sexual relationship. It is important that no details of illicit sex be shown immediately preceding or following the transgression. Passionate fondling and kissing and suggestive postures and gestures should be entirely omitted.

The compensating moral values would require that the principals be made to realize their transgression. Characters associated with the principals must not condone the act. Further, remorse followed by reform and regeneration would need to be shown by both transgressors; or, in the absence of regeneration, some punishment would be necessary to compensate for the wrong done by the principals.

It is evident from a study of these requirements that unless a story introducing a transitory affair is carried thru to a moral conclusion, it may not be treated for the screen. If the plot does not concern itself with the results of the transitory affair, it is apparently better to drop it entirely. An acceptable screen treatment would, of course, be one in which the relationship became the cause of serious consequences to both the transgressors. In that way it would be established that the illicit affair was the cause of subsequent troubles which might have been avoided had not the affair taken place. In other words the thesis would be upheld that one cannot escape the consequences of one's actions even if no one else knows about the transgression, and that punitive events in themselves inevitably take their toll as penalty.

With the dramatization of the troubles resulting from the wrong-doing, the regeneration of the characters would seem an entirely logical development. This is the only type of treatment permissible under the Code principles for any story of this theme intended for the screen.

CHAPTER XXII

MARRIAGE

One of the most noticeable changes which the enforcement of the Production Code has brought about in the treatment of marriage in screen dramas is its restriction in the depiction of the intimacies of married life.

The Code states its position in regard to marital scenes in no uncertain terms. Under the heading of "General Principles," the Code states:

"The sanctity of the institution of marriage and the home shall be upheld. Pictures shall not infer that low forms of sex relationship are the accepted or common thing.

"Pure love, the love of a man for a woman permitted by the law of God and man, is the rightful subject of plots. The passion arising from this love is not the subject for plots.

"Hence, even within the limits of pure love, certain facts have been universally regarded by lawmakers as outside the limits of safe presentation. These are the manifestations of passion and the sacred intimacies or private life, either before marriage in the courtship of decent people; or after marriage, as is perfectly clear.

"In the case of pure love, the difficulty is not so much about what details are permitted for presentation. This is perfectly clear in most cases. The difficulty concerns itself with the tact, delicacy, and general regard for propriety manifested in their presentation."

With an understanding of the Production Code's attitude toward this subject, the reader will find the specific dramatic treatment for themes coming under this classification clarified in the analysis which follows.

Bigamy

Bigamy may be introduced into a screen story, when necessary, but special care is required in its treatment to establish the fact that it is wrong, unlawful, and injurious to the innocent party, as well as that the bigamist is apprehended by the law to be punished for his crime.

Bigamy may, of course, be unintentionally committed; and in that case punishment would not need to be indicated. This may happen in cases where the spouse is believed to be dead and later turns up; or where a divorce believed to be good turns out to be fraudulent for some reason, or other. In such instances the situation is unfortunate, but no one may be charged with a guilty intention.

The only concern of the Code in the treatment of this theme is that bigamy be shown as unlawful and that its unpleasant consequences be indicated when it is committed.

Companionate or Trial Marriage

This type of marriage may never be suggested in a screen story because it represents an attack on traditional marriage and would, consequently, violate that section of the Code which requires that marriage be treated seriously and as an enduring obligation.

Birth Control

The subject of birth control is hardly a suitable one for the screen. Under the Code regulations forbidding themes dealing with "sex education," any theme based on birth control is prohibited for film presentation. This means that it may never be introduced even as an incident in a screen story, either by suggestion or inference.

Honeymoon or First-Night Scenes

Under the Code regulation which states that "Certain facts are regarded as outside the limits of safe presentation," the treatment of honeymoon and first-night scenes is definitely restricted.

A picture could not treat in detail with the reactions and embarrassments suggested by the new relationship of the wedded pair, either immediately prior to, or during their honeymoon. Further, no suggestive discussion or inferences would be permitted regarding such relationship for purposes of comedy, or even, as a matter of fact, for the purpose of serious treatment. The Production Code, and also censor boards in this country and abroad, consider this subject unfit for exhibition before mixed audiences. In England, in particular, first-night scenes are invariably deleted from pictures.

Impotency

A story based upon impotence would have to be rejected under the Production Code, inasmuch as the motion picture cannot serve as the clinic for sex derangements. In this connection, however, the question might be asked, What about historical accuracy in themes dealing with well-known characters? The answer to that is that inasmuch as the characters are so well-known, their very inclusion in the historical tale tells its own story to the adult and requires no further emphasis. In fact, the screen story may not suggest or infer that such a condition exists, but must diligently avoid any reference to the subject in action or dialog.

Marital Relations

The Code warns against "certain facts" regarded as "outside the limits of safe presentation. These are the manifestations of passion and the sacred intimacies of private life."

Under this regulation a picture portraying the intimate marital relations could not be approved. In fact, there should be no dialog or action introduced into a screen story indicative of the marital relationship. Where it is necessary to include bedroom scenes, twin beds should be shown to permit delicate treatment of the implied intimacy.

Polygamy

Polygamy is considered as multiple adultery under the Code, and, therefore any story dealing with this theme must have sufficient compensating moral values to permit its dramatization on the screen. It may not be treated in a favorable or glamorous light, and no details of the intimate life of a colony devoted to polygamy may be portrayed on the screen. It must be shown as illegal, wrong, and subversive of the standards of a Christian society.

Procreation

With the publicity given to wholesale procreation and contests for bigger families in many sections the screen writer is likely to be tempted to dramatize this popular theme.

The subject, however, is one which is difficult to treat in such a way that it would be acceptable for exhibition before mixed audiences. It is easy to see what speculation such a discussion would arouse in the minds of the young and adolescent, not to mention the embarrassment its comedy treatment would cause to many.

The undue emphasis such a picture necessarily throws on the subject of sex is considered generally unwholesome. To many people the suggestion of wholesale mating for commercial gain would be decidedly offensive.

Any story based on this theme would violate that section of the Code which forbids the comedy treatment of sex, and the principle which definitely and specifically forbids showing any pictures which would "tend to arouse morbid curiosity" on the part of the young.

Chapter XXIII

MISCELLANEOUS SEX SUBJECTS

Some sex subjects are so offensive that they can not possibly be treated for the screen; while others are close to the borderline and require careful and delicate treatment to make them acceptable for picturization. These may be listed as follows:

Abortion

Abortion may never be mentioned or even suggested in a screen story. This means that any plot dealing with illegal operations is taboo for the screen.

Childbirth

"Scenes of childbirth, actual or in silhouette are never to be presented," states the Production Code. This means that a film purporting to be a medical treatise would have no place in a public theatre; and no screen story may introduce details of childbirth for dramatization.

Not so very long ago it was not uncommon to see pictures portraying the agony of the mother in the initial stages of parturition. Scenes of this type are both objectionable and offensive, particularly to women, and at the present day both the Code and censor boards everywhere forbid such portrayals.

The depiction of the pains of childbirth are not essential to the motivation of any story. Other alternatives, less offensive, suggest themselves to indicate, if need be, the consequences of painful or prolonged labor which it is sought to establish thru these means.

The Double Standard

The Code recognizes only one standard of morals for both sexes—the highest standard. Therefore the double standard may not be used as a device in screen stories to excuse immorality on the part of the man. It is necessary to introduce the usual compensating moral values whenever any violation of sex morality is indicated, whether the offender be a man or a woman.

Harems

Any story having to do with the more intimate details of a harem, with favorites, eunuchs, slave-girls and concubines would be unacceptable for screen dramatization. Such material is condemned by censor boards in all parts of the world, as well.

The only way in which any reference to a harem might be introduced into a screen story would be in the form of an Arabian Nights fantasy, with no details of the conduct of the harem. The costumes and dances would have to be treated in accordance with the Code regulations specifically relating to *costume* and *dances,* as well as those regulations governing the treatment of sex.

Incest

Incestuous relationships may never be introduced as story material in motion pictures, nor may they be suggested or inferred. Any suggestion of incest automatically disqualifies a story under the Code, and is universally banned by censor boards. It may not be excused in a story on the plea of historical accuracy. Where there is any danger of such an inference, the story must definitely and positively establish the fact that the relationship is an innocent one.

Miscegenation

The Code specifically prohibits miscegenation in its regulation which reads, "Miscegenation (sex relationship between the white and black races) is forbidden." The dictionary defines miscegenation as, "A mixture of races, especially amalgamation of the black and white races."

The Production Code Administration, in interpreting this regulation for application to stories, has regarded miscegenetic unions to be any sex relationship between the white and black races, or in most cases sex union between the white and yellow races. The union of a member of the Polynesians and allied races of the Island groups with a member of the white race is not ordinarily considered a miscegenetic relationship, however. The union of a half-caste of white and Polynesian parentage with a white member would also be exempt from the ruling applying to miscegenation.

Pregnancy

Pregnancy, or expected "blessed events," should never be discussed as such in screen stories. Most censor boards not only frown upon, but almost always delete any such references. Any direct or crude reference to pregnancy in films is considered out-of-place exactly as it would be in any normal society where children are present. It is entirely acceptable, of course, to refer to the baby that is expected, but any reference to conception, child-bearing, and child-birth is considered improper for public discussion.

Rape

The Code specifically states that "Rape is a difficult subject and bad material from the viewpoint of the general audience in the theatre," and gives the following regulations for its treatment:

1. It should never be introduced as subject matter unless absolutely essential to the plot.
2. It should never be treated as comedy.
3. Where essential to the plot, it must not be more than *suggested*.
4. Even the struggles preceding rape should not be shown.

Rape is very rarely permitted as an element in a screen story. The screenplay must be a very unusual one, and have strong compensating moral values before the suggestion of this enormous crime is allowed under the Code for dramatization. The acceptability of any screen story of this kind on social, ethical and moral grounds would have to be decided specifically by the Production Code Administration. The writer who uses this subject in his story, therefore, has no assurance that the screenplay will be accepted, irrespective of its manner of treatment, since so many other factors enter into a judgment of the theme.

Sale of Women

The sale or barter of a woman for immoral purposes is forbidden for portrayal in a screen story. This means that care must be taken that no such suggestion is given even in stories dealing with the sale of slaves in periods of the past. Generally, the sale of a woman, whether in a public market or in private, is considered improper and objectionable for screen dramatization.

Sex Perversion

No hint of sex perversion may be introduced into a screen story. The characterization of a man as effeminate, or a woman as grossly masculine would be absolutely forbidden for screen portrayal. This means, too, that no comedy character may be introduced into a screen play pantomiming a pervert.

White Slavery

White slavery may never be referred to even by suggestion in a screen story. The Code definitely prohibits this subject in its regulation which reads, "White slavery shall not be treated." Any attempt to introduce it in pictures in the guise of "sex hygiene," is also forestalled by the regulation that "Sex hygiene and venereal diseases are not subjects for motion pictures."

Chapter XXIV

PROSTITUTION

The general provisions outlined below as representing the required "compensating moral values," for the treatment of the theme of prostitution on the screen do not in themselves constitute the basis for a judgment as to the story's acceptability. A story may meet all these requirements and still be unacceptable for screen dramatization. Each story is subject to individual scrutiny under the industry's "good will and welfare" clause. This attitude is taken because of the dangerous element of suggestion inherent in the theme, the total effects of which can only be determined by an examination of the complete story.

One thing is certain, there will never be a cycle of pictures based on this theme, irrespective of the popularity of any one film. The Production Code Administration uses its prerogatives in the interests of the commonweal to withhold any subjects which it deems subversive of public morals.

The analysis of this theme is, therefore, merely intended to indicate the *trend* of the plot necessary under the Code, and to suggest the aspects of it which are wholly forbidden for dramatization. The "compensating moral values" which comprise the test of the basic story dealing with prostitution are as follows:

1. It must be established that prostitution is *wrong*.
2. No details of the *business* of prostitution should be given at any time.

3. No profit may be shown to accrue from prostitution.
4. The condonation, glorification, or acceptance of a prostitute, or of prostitution, should never be suggested.
5. Prostitution must be definitely and affirmatively condemned as wrong by sympathetic characters.
6. Ample compensating moral values must be introduced by way of punishment and stigma.

The following provisions of the Code are also of interest in connection with this theme:

"Brothels and houses of ill-fame, no matter of what country, are not proper locations for drama. They suggest to the average person at once sex sin, or they excite an unwholesome and morbid curiosity in the minds of youth. In general, they are dangerous and bad dramatic locations."

Analysis

The first and last provisions that "Prostitution must be shown to be wrong," and that "there must be ample compensating moral values by way of punishment and stigma," indicate that the screen story must be treated as a tragedy, or, at best, it is necessarily confined to a tragic ending.

The theme would, therefore, be that "Prostitution is committed and brings suffering, punishment and stigma," and the thesis would have to be that, "An evil past cannot be lived down, but always and inevitably arises to confound the wrong-doer."

The treatment of the plot is restricted by the second provision which states that "No details of the business of prostitution should be given," and by the third provision which specifically states that "No profit may be shown to accrue from prostitution." These prohibit a picture from showing a prostitute *operating* as a prostitute, or profiting from prostitution. In addition, it means that no locale suggestive of a brothel or house of ill-fame, or its sophisticated counterpart, a "house of assignation," may be shown in films, even where such a place is combined with a gambling establishment or other type of deceptive "front." The habitation of the prostitute, too, must not give the impression that she is engaged in the business of prostitution. There must be no details of such operation even in a private residence. Further, there should be no characters in the story which might be identified as inmates ordinarily associated with houses of prostitution of whatever category. Any locale suggestive of a brothel or house of ill-fame is forbidden by the specific Code regulation which states that such locales "are *not* proper locations for drama."

Condonation

The fourth provision that "The condonation, glorification, or acceptance of a prostitute should never be suggested" is intended to prohibit plots in which a "justifiable" motive for prostitution is offered. The commonplace plots that come within this category are those of mother love, with its sentimental appeal of self-sacrifice; the love of a daughter for her parents; the affection of a sister for her brother; bankruptcy, financial stringency, and poverty.

The attempt to us any such "motive" in a screen story is definitely forbidden. The Code does not allow the justification of prostitution for any reason and under any pretext of worthiness, since this would violate the regulation which states that "No picture should lower the moral standards of those who see it," and which, according to the Code, is done when "Evil is made to appear attractive [as it is when prostitution is made to appear a form of commendable self-sacrifice] and good is made to appear unattractive [as when it is indicated that it is harder and less pleasant to earn a living by honest toil than by prostitution]; and when the sympathy of the audience is thrown on the side of crime, wrong-doing and evil [as it obviously is when prostitution is justified for sentimental reasons, or unfavorable economic conditions]."

This provision prohibits a screen story from glorifying the life of a prostitute by making it appear attractive, desirable, glamorous or thrilling.

Further no characters in the story may indicate sympathy for the prostitute or condone her evil life. No tacit approval or acceptance of prostitution by anyone can be shown.

Condemnation

The provisions of the Code do not stop merely with the prohibition of condonation or approval of prostitution, but require, as set forth in the fifth provision, that "Prostitution must be definitely and affirmatively condemned as wrong by sympathetic characters."

This provision has been added because of the frequent tendency in stories of this kind to indicate condemnation of the prostitute, and prostitution, from a source wholly unsympathetic in nature. If this were to be allowed in a screen story, the general impression would be created that a prostitute is punished and "persecuted" only by the "narrow-minded," by busybodies, or by smug, contemptible hypocrites. The Code does not permit a story to characterize the decent element of the community in this unjust fashion.

Consequently, sympathetic, wholesome and likeable characters, representative of the average normal man and woman, must condemn prostitution as a great evil, and the prostitute as a misguided, erring woman.

Incidental Characterization

The prostitute as an incidental character in a screen story is definitely banned from the screen except in such a case where it is evident that the entire story hinges upon the incident. It may be allowed under such a condition if the story, in itself, is thoroly acceptable in all other respects. The judgment as to the acceptability of such an incidental characterization could not, of course, be decided by anyone but the Production Code Administration.

In the unusual instance where the incidental prostitute is permitted in a screen story, she must never be shown "soliciting," on the street, or elsewhere, since this detail is prohibited by the provision forbidding "the business of prostitution." It must be established, too, that she has no sex relations with any character in the story. If there is any danger of *suggesting* that she has relations of this kind, the entire incident would be automatically rejected for screen presentation, since there is no opportunity in such an "incidental" characterization to introduce the necessary "compensating moral values" required by the Code.

The prostitute could not, of course, be made an attractive character, and condemnation would have to be voiced somewhere in the story against the prostitute and prostitution.

CHAPTER XXV

SEDUCTION

Seduction, as defined by the dictionary and as understood by the Code is, "Enticing a chaste woman to illicit sexual intercourse by a promise of marriage or by other means of persuasion, without the use of force. When a married man is involved, seduction is also adultery."

Since the enforcement of the Code, very few stories have been made dealing with this theme, because seduction may no longer be introduced as an "incident," and then forgotten. It must be carried thru to a moral conclusion.

The following "compensating moral values" are required under the Code:

1. When introduced as part of the basic plot, seduction can never be more than suggested; and it must never be detailed in method or manner.
2. Seduction must not be presented in such a way as to arouse passion or morbid curiosity on the part of the spectator.
3. Seduction must not be presented as attractive and beautiful.
4. Seduction must never be justified—or be made to seem right and permissible under any circumstances.
5. Thruout the presentation right and wrong should never be confused. From the moment that seduction is introduced to the end of the story, it must be definitely established that it is wrong and sinful, and that it brings condemnation and suffering. There must be suffering and reform, or **punishment.**

Seduction must always be treated as a serious subject. The Code definitely says that it "should *never* be treated as comedy."

The compensating moral values may be introduced into the screen story as suggested in the following analysis of the regulations.

1. *The seduction must never be detailed in method or manner*

In the words of the Code, "The methods by which seduction, essential to the plot, is attained, should not be explicit or represented in detail where there is likelihood of arousing wrongful emotions on the part of the audience."

The most common dramatic devices used in fiction are the very ones which are prohibited under the Code by this regulation. In an ordinary story the heroine may be baldly—or delicately—approached and "propositioned." If the hero meets with refusal, he may batter down her resistance by whatever art of persuasion he has at his command. In a screen story, however, none of these devices may be used. It is felt that such details, aside from the fact that they might tend to be instructive in wrong-doing, are out of place for exhibition before mixed audiences in theatres.

Consequently, seduction may never be introduced unless absolutely essential for the basic plot, and, even then, it may never be more than *suggested*.

2. *Seduction must not be presented in a way to arouse passion or morbid curiosity*

The Code regulations state that:

Because of the natural and spontaneous reaction of normal human beings to sexual stimuli, the portrayal of definite manifestations of sex (such as details of love-making, passionate kissing and fondling) is harmful to individual morality and subversive to the interests of society (by the possibility of arousing sex excitement in the spectator).

For this reason, while an ordinary story or play might deal with the details of love-making, these details would be forbidden in a screen story because:

> First—Physical contact must be kept at a minimum in stories dealing with illicit sex. At no point of the drama (either before or after the illicit affair) can excessive and passionate kissing, embracing or other physical contact be indulged in.

> Second—What little physical contact is required for the plot motivation must not be enacted with the characters in a horizontal position, or within suggestive proximity of beds, lounges, or deserted and secluded fields.

3. *Seduction must not be presented as something attractive*

In a screen story seduction may never be dramatized in a way to make it appear either attractive or profitable. Even if the story ends with the marriage of the principals, it would require, first, the introduction of the "compensating moral values" of suffering, remorse, repentance and regeneration of both transgressors. According to the provisions of the Code dealing with this aspect:

"No picture should lower the moral standards of those who see it:

This is done *when evil is made to appear attractive*" (as when seduction is shown to result in profit, pleasure or happiness)
"And good is made to appear unattractive."
(As it would be if this way goodness, purity, and honor are made to seem of negligible value, and when it is in-

dicated that happiness may be more easily gained by "easy virtue.")

With dramatization of the wrong, and the unhappy consequences which follow, the Code believes that the ill-effects of seduction are shown to far outweigh its brief pleasures for both the transgressors, and that it is, therefore, presented without any false glamour.

The provision that seduction must not be presented as something attractive is intended to limit, too, the scenes showing the development of the love affair which culminates in the seduction, so that they will not be invested with too much romance or glamour. The Code regulations governing this point state:

"The presentation of evil is often essential for drama. This in itself is not wrong, provided that *evil is not presented alluringly.* Even if later on the evil is condemned or punished, it must not be allowed to appear so attractive that the emotions are drawn to desire or approve so strongly that later they forget the condemnation and remember only the apparent joy of the sin."

4. *Seduction must never be justified*

In a screen story, the Code allows no excuse or justification of seduction for any reason whatever. Even though it may be claimed that the principals were "carried away" by their love for each other, the offense is not thereby justified. Further, since the Code recognizes no "double standard" of morals, the man's guilt may not be exonerated under that head.

If seduction becomes the basis for a plot introducing illegitimacy, promiscuity, adultery, or prostitution, the Code requires that these concurrent subjects conform to the specific regulations and provisions governing their individual treatment for the screen. This means that seduction may not be used as a justification for subsequent immoralities of whatever nature or extent.

The Code believes that to justify seduction would be to "Throw the sympathy of the audience on the side of wrong-doing and evil." Therefore, it must be condemned as wrong by sympathetic and sincere characters, and by all those closely associated with the principals; it must never be condoned, nor must indifference to it be indicated on the part of anyone.

4. *There must be suffering and reform, or punishment*

The Code provides that:

> "Wrong-doing, evil and sin need not always be punished so long as the audience is made to know it is wrong."

In a theme of seduction, the suffering and remorse of both transgressors, and the effort on the man's part to right the wrong he has done, will be sufficient to cancel the wrong and the story may end happily. If, however, there is no remorse and regeneration, and no restitution is made, the seducer must be shown, not only to suffer, but some form of punishment must also be meted out to him to compensate for the wrong he has done. As stated previously, the girl, of course, should be shown to suffer sufficiently from the condemnation and stigma resulting from the sin to compensate for her transgression. Further punishment would not be necessary in her case.

Chapter XXVI

THE TRIANGLE

The Code regulations specifically state that, "The triangle, that is, the love of a third party by one already married, needs careful handling, if marriage, the sanctity of the home, and sex morality are not to be imperilled."

The Code, in seeking to uphold the sanctity of marriage, considers any attempt to *justify* the triangle, even where it does not involve adultery, as the type of treatment which would "throw sympathy against marriage as an institution." This would be particularly the case in a story which would justify the outside emotional interest of a married person because of the disinterest or mistreatment received at the hands of the marriage partner. The Code takes the attitude that any dramatization which appears to justify the triangle ignores the question of marital responsibility and suggests that this irresponsible concept of marital obligations is common and "acceptable."

Practically the same regulations apply to the theme of the triangle as to adultery, except that it need not be dramatized as a tragedy, and, since there is no actual transgression, there is no need to show suffering and punishment.

If, for instance, the story were to concern a very unpleasant husband who mistreats his wife, the audience would look upon the husband as the "villain" of the piece. No matter how righteous an individual he might be, his characterization as a scoundrel would make the wife a martyr. If the wife were to be shown seeking attentions while married, the fact that she is characterized as a martyr would make the audience sympathize with her extra-marital interests and thus throw their sympathy on the side of "wrong-doing."

To consider another possible development of the above situation, it would be acceptable, so far as the Code is concerned, to characterize the wife as *fickle*, and as turning to an outsider for attention. But the husband could not, in this case, be made a very unpleasant individual, because if he were to be so characterized, it would appear to give the wife a good reason to seek attentions outside the home, and in this way the audience would be led to believe that it is perfectly acceptable in such circumstances to violate the moral obligations and vows of marriage. This impression could easily be avoided by characterizing the husband in this situation either as a likeable, wholesome chap who does his best to make his marriage a success, and fails to please his wife thru no fault of his own; or, if necessary to the plot, he could be shown as a rather reserved and cool person, who is a *good husband* but not a demonstrative one. In either instance the audience sympathy would be with the husband and with his efforts *to save his marriage*. Disapproval, on the other hand, would be felt for the wife's irresponsible and fickle attitude, and thus "wrong would be definitely characterized as wrong." The sanctity of marriage and the home would be upheld.

If it were required for the plot that neither the husband nor the wife be characterized in an unsympathetic light, it would be perfectly acceptable to make both of them charming and pleasant persons, on good terms with one another. The third party, in this case, might be introduced as an unscrupulous character who succeeds in "turning the head" of the husband or wife, and in this way alienating him, or her, from the marriage partner. The sympathy of the audience would obviously be with the deserted mate, and not with the other characters.

Whatever form the treatment takes, the third party should never be characterized as a very sympathetic person, because, if he is, it would be difficult to create audience disapproval of his actions in breaking up the home.

In stories of this sort, kissing or fondling between the erring pair should either not be shown at all, or held at a minimum.

With characterization of the principals so developed as to create audience sympathy for the right, and disapproval for the wrong, the story should include, in addition, some other individual representing the "voice of morality" to condemn the wrong being done by the two responsible for the triangle.

The Single Standard

Differing pointedly from ordinary dramatic procedure, a screen story would have to establish the fact that the marriage is binding, morally, on both the wife and the husband. The Code considers a husband's irresponsible attitude toward marriage as reprehensible as a wife's. Thus a wife may not condone her husband's peregrinations on the basis that "after all, he's a man." The story should indicate her displeasure with his actions. She must not be shown to remain indifferent to the situation.

Divorce

If divorce is necessary to the dramatization of the story, its disruptive effects upon the home and the family should be shown—especially if there are children.

The Ending

If a happy ending is desired for a story based on the triangle, the following provisions should be met:

If separation has only been *threatened* by infatuation for the third party, reconciliation between husband and wife could readily take place. Inasmuch as no sin has been committed, and no wrong has actually been done, the husband's or wife's expressed regret for his or her actions would be sufficient to compensate for the temporary alienation. No specific treatment of the third party is necessary in such a case. If the plot takes a slightly different turn, and it would be desirable to bring in the third party, this party might be made to realize the wrong being done to the family by the breakup of the marriage, or the alienation of the affections, and might be urged to remove himself from the domestic scene before any serious consequences develop.

If separation actually occurs thru an alienation of affection, and a breakup of the home follows with divorce, these serious consequences would require showing that the fickle mate and the third party suffer in some way to compensate for the wrong which has been done. This would not be difficult because the story would have established earlier that one or both of these individuals is a rather unpleasant person, and it would be logical to assume that they could not make each other happy. With one of them irresponsible and the other unscrupulous, the punishment suggests itself.

Analysis

Because of the infinite variations of the theme, it would not be possible to suggest the treatment of each. However, the writer may readily determine whether his story fulfills the basic requirements of the Code by a simple analysis suggested below.

1. FIRST DETERMINE WHAT THE PROBLEM IS

   In the "triangle," the problem is usually one of domestic difficulties; loss of interest in the marriage partner; or a fickle nature, demanding new emotional experiences.

2. DETERMINE WHETHER OR NOT THE MOTIVE FOR THE ACTION IS HONORABLE

   The husband's or wife's motive in seeking, or accepting, outside attentions is, obviously, not honorable.

   The third party's motive in alienating the affections of a married person is patently dishonorable.

   Both motives are detrimental in that they violate the sanctity of the marriage and the home.

3. DETERMINE THE HONORABLE SOLUTION TO THE PROBLEM PRESENTED

   Domestic difficulties are honorably solved by the cooperation and compromise of the husband and wife.

   Where, for some reason or other, the difficulties or differences can not be solved in this way, the law provides the alternative of separation or divorce.

   These are the only honorable means of solving a domestic problem.

The characterization of the principals is disclosed by this analysis. Apparently the characters in the story who employ dishonorable means to secure their ends must be shown in their true light. If these dishonorable actions succeed in breaking up the home, the characters responsible for this wrong must be punished.

The "voice of morality" should *express* in the story the correct solution of the problem *by honorable means,* so that, even if the dénouement is a breakup of the marriage, the audience will know not only that this wrongdoing has brought suffering and punishment, but will also be made to understand what the rightful solution of the problem is according to honorable and fair standards of conduct. This point can be established by dialog, where necessary. It may also be introduced by any other dramatic devices which will lend themselves to the development of the individual plot.

GENERAL PICTURE SUBJECTS

CHAPTER XXVII

GENERAL SUBJECTS

Certain subjects, concerning which the Code has made specific provisions in its regulations, and those which present important problems in screen dramatization, are dealt with in this chapter under the following headings:

Animals in Films	Profanity
Army, Navy and Marines	Religion
	Suicide
Drinking and Drunkenness	Vulgarity
	Foreign Nations in Pictures
Geographical and Historical Subjects	

Any indication of cruelty to animals in a picture is sufficient to ban it from the English picture market. The strict regulations concerning the treatment of enlisted men in the Service have put an end to the old-time films dealing with the brawls and debaucheries of soldiers and sailors in foreign ports, which formerly provided the theme for most of these stories. Drinking is indulged in to a much milder extent; but only those who understand the unceasing work of the Production Code Administration to minimize such scenes can grasp the full extent of the progress made by the industry in this connection. Nudity has been largely exempted from the screen by the enforcement of the Code regulations in the travel films dealing with native life. Profanity has been entirely banned from pictures; and religion receives its due reverence as never before. No longer may a Minister of the Gospel be characterized as a moral weakling, a hypocrite, or a scoundrel hiding behind the protection of the cloth.

CHAPTER XXVIII

ANIMALS IN FILMS

Cruelty to Animals

No story intended for the screen should ever introduce any episode or scene showing cruelty to animals in any form, or for any reason. Such portrayal is disallowed under the provisions of the Production Code relating to "brutality, horror and gruesomeness."

The British Board of Censors in London is particularly concerned with the indication of cruelty to animals in pictures. The following interesting commentary gives the Board's rulings in this regard:

"The inclusion in films of animals, both domestic and wild, has always received the most careful consideration of the Board since its inception in 1912. Its members appreciate, to the full, the tremendous amount of voluntary effort that has been expended in this country during the last century for the purpose of inculcating a spirit of kindness and consideration towards dumb animals. . . . Bearing these considerations in mind, it was felt that it would be inadmissable to permit on the screen incidents which would be likely to undermine all that had been done for the welfare of dumb animals. Moreover, it is realized that it would be most unwholesome for children, especially those of tender years, to witness acts of cruelty on the screen, as the cumulative effect of such incidents would undermine their moral character. Consequently, it has always been the practice of the Board not to certificate any film depicting cruelty to animals."

With the foregoing principles in mind, the British Board of Censors arrived at the following conclusions, made public in an annual report:

"First: That it must maintain its standard of not allowing any incident on the screen depicting cruelty. If scenes in a film are introduced with the object of showing pain or suffering on the part of an animal, whether such pain is caused by accident or intention, such scenes are *prima facie* censorable. Indeed, we do not allow any incident, however innocent it may be, if it conveys the idea of cruelty.

"Second: That it could not allow any incident, if it could reasonably be supposed to have been produced by means which necessitated cruelty, or restraint amounting to cruelty. . . . It has been argued that films should be allowed which are genuine representations of what actually takes place in nature, and where there is clear proof that the scenes are in no way 'staged.' Even then we have taken up the position that we cannot allow harrowing or revolting details."

Since most of the films produced in this country are made with an eye to the British market, the writer would do well to keep his story within the bounds demanded by the British Board of Censors.

The branding of animals would come under this head, and therefore no visual details should be given. Where it is necessary to the plot to indicate branding, it can be merely suggested.

Rats and Snakes

The Code restricts, under the regulations governing "horror and gruesomeness," the use of these animals for purposes of dramatization.

References to rats are considered at all times "poor theatre," and they should never be introduced visually into a story even for purposes of plot motivation. The horror and fear which the sight of them arouses in the spectator, and particularly in children, is considered definitely harmful.

A scientific picture may show snakes in their normal habitat. Other pictures may show snakes only where they are absolutely necessary for proper plot motivation. Even in this case, however, they should not be introduced too often.

Vivisection

Under the Code regulations relating to "horror and gruesomeness," the *details* of vivisection could not be permitted in a screen story. However, vivisection may sometimes be a necessary part of a plot. When this is the case, the presence of the animals may be indicated. The purpose for which they are to be used, however, should never be more than *suggested*, specifically in the dialog. This means, of course, that no scene may appear in a picture actually showing the vivisection of an animal.

CHAPTER XXIX

THE ARMY, NAVY AND MARINES

The Production Code is not alone in its insistence upon certain restrictions to be observed in stories which deal with soldiers, sailors and marines. A Federal statute—U. S. Code Title 10, Section 1393—governs the use of "The uniform of the U. S. Army, Navy or Marine Corps in any playhouse or theatre, or in motion picture films."

This law provides that the character in a screen story wearing the uniform of the Army, Navy, or Marine Corps must not be represented in such a manner as to "bring discredit or reproach upon the U. S. Army, Navy or Marine Corps." The law provides further that "Any person who offends against the provisions of this section shall, on conviction, be punished by a fine not exceeding three hundred dollars, or by imprisonment not exceeding six months, or by both such fine and imprisonment."

The officials of the War Department formally advised the motion picture industry that "The outstanding cause for complaint is the injection of the naval enlisted man's uniform into 'dive' scenes to provide 'atmosphere.' The picturization of enlisted men as 'hardboiled,' ignorant, heavy-drinking, and woman-chasers is also deplored. Another practice objected to is the tendency to play upon the dignity of high naval rank to develop comedy. The law permits the wearing of the uniform by moving picture actors representing naval characters, 'provided their characterization does not bring discredit or reproach

upon the United States Army, Navy or Marine Corps.'
The War Department desires the proper presentation of
naval traditions and activities on the screen. It is not the
desire of the Navy to have the Navy man pictured as a
saint or without human failings, but it is felt that pictures go entirely too far the other way."

It was also stated that "Not only does such picturization create in the minds of many a reproachful conception
of the personnel of the Navy, but reacts against the
Department's efforts to recruit for the service the best
available material from the youth of the country."

In accordance with the regulations of the Production
Code, any story dealing with soldiers, sailors or marines
must be careful not to introduce episodes dealing with
prostitutes, brothels, dives, or houses of prostitution.
Further, the introduction of drunken brawls is restricted
under the regulations forbidding "excessive drinking and
drunkenness." It is obvious from these rulings, as well
as the Federal statute relating to pictures of the Service,
that a story intended for screen dramatization must treat
of the reputable activities of soldiers, sailors or marines.

War Department Cooperation

It would be impractical for the motion picture industry to attempt to make pictures without the aid of the
Service. Definite rules, therefore, have been established
by the War Department in this connection:

> "Army cooperation is extended only under condition:
> "a) That the picture depict American soldiers, cadets,
> or scenes which require a true interpretation of
> Army life, represent incidents in which the Army
> was engaged, or have some historical or educational
> value from an Army viewpoint.
> "b) That the picture does not involve the use of military
> personnel in a depiction of the soldiers of other
> nations."

"Navy cooperation is extended only under the following conditions:

"a) This picture must not have as its background the life and activities of a foreign navy.

"b) No vessel of the U.S. Navy will be photographed or shown as under any other flag than our own, nor will naval personnel be permitted to impersonate the personnel of another service.

"c) The picture must contain nothing which tends in any way to discredit any branch of the government, or any foreign government service, or the personnel or uniform of such services.

"d) The picture must not contain anything offensive to public morals or good taste, or be otherwise objectionable."

CHAPTER XXX

DRINKING AND DRUNKENNESS

The Code specifically states:

"The use of liquor should never be excessively presented even in picturing countries where its use is legal. In scenes from American life, the necessities of plot and proper characterization alone justify its use, and in this case, it should be shown with moderation."

After a repeal of prohibition, drinking became common in films, not because of any dramatic value inherent in drinking, but chiefly to provide action and movement during dialog. Thus drinking was usually introduced as a prelude, interlude, and postlude to long-winded conversations.

The public groups, however, voted "thumbs down" on continuous imbibing in pictures, and particularly on "drunks." In response to this demand, the Production Code Administration issued the edict that "Drinking must be reduced to the minimum," and clarified this regulation as follows:

"The complaint is not so much against drinking when necessary for the plot, as, for instance, when a character is portrayed definitely as an unfortunate drunkard, or is driven to drink by circumstances inherent in the story. What is objected to is the incessant 'smart' drinking indulged in by the otherwise straight leads in pictures, apart from any story demands, or the exaggerated use of drinking for comedy purposes.

"Frequently this type of action is injected principally to garnish or liven up a scene which otherwise would be mainly dialog. It is felt that some other type of action other than drinking could easily be devised to high-light scenes."

This regulation reinstated the Code restrictions on drinking which had been in force during prohibition, and which, upon the repeal of prohibition, were more or less disregarded by producers in the belief that drinking was no longer "against the law."

The writer, in preparing any screen story, must keep in mind that drinking—or drunkenness—may never be introduced except for purposes of plot motivation, and even in such a case it "should be shown with moderation." This means that the comic drunken character is no longer acceptable when injected merely to provide comedy; excessive drinking and maudlin drunkenness are forbidden both by the Code and by censor boards everywhere, because of its effect on young people who see in such portrayals the suggestion that drinking is "smart," and the acceptable thing to do. The publicity which has been given to the fact that most traffic accidents are due to drinking, and the indication that drinking tends toward an increase of immorality and crime of all kinds are largely responsible for the public attitude against popularizing drinking in pictures.

The Code restrictions would apply with particular force in any story where women are shown as drunk, as such a suggestion is considered decidedly offensive, and such characterizations should, therefore, be avoided.

CHAPTER XXXI

GEOGRAPHICAL AND HISTORICAL SUBJECTS

The attitude of the Production Code Administration towards geographical and historical themes with relation to the Code regulations is clearly manifest in its comment quoted below:

"Morals laid down in the Code cannot be altered on the ground of geographical or historical incident. A wrong recorded as true in history and artistically treated in a classic may not, for that reason, be exempted from the test of the Code. Nor may repulsive and obscene practices of savage tribes of our own day be shown on the screen merely because they are true and considered proper in the jungle.

"This rule, however, does not mean that all themes, plots, and treatments are judged under the Code as if they were of today. Such procedure would lack common sense and would be unworkable. Obviously, for example, law and order can not be expected to prevail in the historic Wild West. It is evident, furthermore, that Shakespeare and Eugene O'Neill can not be judged exactly alike. Again, the evil usages of a bygone age, no longer practiced, are not subject to the same censorship as modern ways and customs. In general, historic and older classical subjects possess a certain quality of distance and unreality which mitigate effects which would be evil in a similar modern subject."

Under the Code regulations, the details of sex and crime, horror and cruelty in historical and geographical stories are subject to the same restrictions as are these subjects in modern stories. Obviously these evils manifest themselves in the same form as in the past, and in their case, consequently, it is not true that "distance and unreality" is capable of mitigating their evil effects today. Only those "evil usages *no longer practiced*" are allowed a wider latitude in films, though even these must be subject always, of course, to the dictates of good taste.

South Sea Island Stories

In compliance with the rules stated above, any stories with a South Sea locale may not, because of their geographical location, be exempted from the regulations of the Code dealing with sex and crime. Because of the frequency of depicting missionaries in such stories, those provisions of the Code are applicable which state that "no film or episode may throw ridicule on any religious faith," and that "Ministers of religion in their character as ministers of religion should not be used as *comic characters, or as villains*."

Sexual immorality among the natives, or any suggestion of illicit sex in the relations of whites with natives is not permissible for treatment in a film story. The regulations regarding illicit sex, prostitution, seduction, and rape apply to South Sea Island stories, as well as to stories of other locales.

The Code rules forbidding miscegenation would need to be observed in stories introducing either the relation or marriage of whites to either the black or yellow races. Strictly speaking "miscegenation" is "a mixture of races"; but the Code intention is to characterize as a miscegenetic union any relation between the white race and the black and in most cases also between the white and the yellow races. Consequently unions between natives of other than these races with whites would not, for Code purposes, be considered as "miscegenation."

The specific story, however, would have to be judged on its merits by the Production Code Administration, as there may be unusual exceptions, particularly where the individual is a half-caste, with a mixture of races, and where it would not be possible to determine the classification in which the character fits, by any cursory examination.

Travelogues

Because nudity or semi-nudity is common and customary among the natives of savage tribes, Code exemption is often claimed on the excuse that such portrayals are "true-to-life." However, again under the ruling in regard to "geographical" subjects, travelogues must be treated with regard for the Code regulations prohibiting nudity in fact, or silhouette, and particularly the exposure of women's breasts. Scenes which show nude children exposing sex organs are also forbidden by the Code and hence may not be portrayed even in a travelogue.

CHAPTER XXXII

PROFANITY

In accordance with the Code provisions relating to profanity, the name of the Deity shall never be used except in instances where it is necessary and sacred. It may not, however, be used *indiscriminately* even by ministers or priests.

No suggestion may be given in a screen play that a character is *"swearing under his breath."* Further, *any movement of the lips suggestive of profanity* is prohibited. *Unfinished sentences* suggestive of profanity are not permitted in film stories; nor may *foreign terms* for Deity, or foreign sentences suggestive of profanity be used in pictures, even though they may be understandable to only part of the audience.

The following words are forbidden by the Code:

Damn, God-damn, Goddam, damn you, etc.

God, by God, for God's sake, God in heaven, etc.

Christ, for Christ's sake, Cripes, etc.

Jesus (or any corrupted words derived from this name such as "Jeez," "Geez," etc.)

Hell, from hell to breakfast, Oh! hell, hell and damnation, etc.

Lord, Oh, my Lord, Good Lord, Lord in heaven, Lordy, Lawdy.

Son-of-a-B——.

The intent of the Code is to forbid all profane and blasphemous words, and their corruptions.

Chapter XXXIII

RELIGION

The Code states:

1. No film or episode may throw *ridicule* on any religious faith.
2. Ministers of religion in their character as ministers of religion should not be used as comic characters or villains.
3. Ceremonies of any definite religion should be carefully and respectfully handled.

It goes on to eludicate that:

> "The reason why ministers of religion may not be comic characters or villains is simply because the attitude taken toward them may easily become the attitude taken toward religion in general. Religion is lowered in the minds of the audience because of the lowering of the audience's respect for a minister."

These provisions prohibit making comedy characters out of ministers; or dramatizing the minister as other than a venerable character, so long as he is portrayed as a minister of religion. Not only may a minister not be characterized as a villain, but he may not be shown to fall from grace or to commit any sin or crime. Under these regulations a character such as appeared in "Rain," could not be portrayed on the screen.

British Regulations on Religion

Inasmuch as the British regulations in regard to religious subjects are very strict, and as much of the

American product is intended for exhibition in England, almost all pictures are made to comply with their provisions.

The British do not permit comedy in a church, and for this reason many of the recent pictures introducing comical events taking place during weddings have shown the marriage ceremony taking place at the home of a Justice of the Peace, who, being only a civil authority, can be interrupted as often as is required for the development of the hectic plot.

Sir Edward Shortt, in a report, has given the following rules in regard to the religious phase of pictures intended for exhibition in England:

"As you can well imagine, the greatest care must be exercised in subjects dealing, however reverently, with religious views, and the practise of religious rites. We frequently have many anxious hours over stories which are beautifully carried out, lest we should run the risk of touching on the sacred and delicate ground of religious feeling. Both of my predecessors established the standard, with which I heartily agree, that no incident shall be passed which is likely to offend the just susceptibilities of any religious section of the community.

". . . We have to be particularly careful in the representation of the Sacraments of any of the established churches. For this reason, scenes of christenings, marriages and funerals have to be, so far as the words of the services are concerned, reduced to a minimum. Under no circumstances do we allow a farce or knock-about comedy to be enacted in what is represented as a place of public worship, and several films have been rejected on this account. Comic incidents at a baptism, wedding or funeral are quite out of place, and are always deleted. . . . Such incidents are quite unsuitable for public exhibition in this country.

"The situation of what is and what is not permitted to pass on the screen with regard to religious ceremonies, depends largely on the treatment and environment of such ceremonies. The following are standard rulings:

(1) Any ceremony that takes place in church or in any similar sacred building must be treated in a reverent manner, because it takes place on consecrated ground.

Comedy is allowed to pass in civil marriages. The marriage ceremony in 'The Bride Comes Home' would not have been permitted had it taken place in a church.

(2) The parts of a service that are invariably deleted are as follows:

    (a) The actual Blessing given in the Lord's name; i.e. 'In the name of the Father, the Son and the Holy Ghost.'

    (b) The actual part of a ceremony which constitutes the sacramental element; that is the giving of Holy Communion and Absolution, e.g. the scene in 'Scarlet Empress' where the priest lays a wafer on the tongues of the people he marries.

(3) There is a standing objection to the Lord's prayer, and it is invariably deleted, whether spoken by a Minister or a layman, in church or out of church, reverently or not—treatment has nothing to do with it—it must come out."

Religious Prejudice

Under the regulations of the Code no picture could be made which would make an issue of religious differences, or indicate violence being done to any individual or group because of religious prejudices. Such elements may not be introduced into a screen play, since they would tend to ridicule a particular faith.

Religious Workers

Under the same ruling which forbids portraying a Minister of religion as a comic character or as a villain, no girl or woman portrayed as a religious worker may be characterized in any way which would reflect upon religion. This means that she could be portrayed only as an upstanding, moral and sympathetic character. By the term "religious worker" is meant a person having a direct connection with some religion, representing a

Church or religious organization. A social worker would not, of course, be included in this category.

Mae West, in the much discussed picture, "Klondike Annie," portrayed a social settlement worker in Alaska. Many people, however, mistook her garb to be that of a religious worker, and the songs sung in the Settlement House to be hymns sung by a "congregation." It was this impression which created much of the public censure of this picture.

CHAPTER XXXIV

SUICIDE

Crime

First and foremost, the Code regulations in regard to suicide are intended to restrict its use as a device to cheat the law. Therefore criminals may not be shown committing suicide to evade punishment for their crimes. Where it is necessary for the plot to indicate the death of the criminal, accidental death might be suggested in place of suicide.

The only exception to the rule is in the case of an insane person. If insanity is definitely established as the reason for the criminal act, then suicide might be introduced, since it might be argued that the insane man was not in full possession of his reason and therefore was not mentally—hence not morally—responsible for the acts of suicide or the crime preceding it.

However, suicide may never be suggested as an attempted evasion of legal punishment, since it is not considered as having sufficient moral value to compensate for the crime or evil which has been done. Punishment of the criminal alone satisfies the requirement of "compensating moral value," where accidental death is not introduced when essential to the proper motivation of the plot. In many states attempted suicide is a criminal offense in itself.

General

In cases of moral offenses, the pregnancy of an unmarried mother, marital discords, and other personal problems, suicide is considered as an immoral act, and not as a proper solution in a screen story. The alarming frequency of suicide in real life makes such a suggestion in pictures doubly dangerous in its social consequences. For this reason suicide is permitted only in unusual circumstances, and where its inclusion in a story marks the climax of cumulative suffering and punishment. Thus it is evident that suicide may not be used as an "escape" by any character in the screen story at the first hint of retribution for wrongs which have been committed, to terminate a life of sin or crime; or as a self-righteous effort to avenge hurt pride in marital or family discords.

Suicide, in itself, is not considered as having any "compensating moral value," and therefore may never be used as a form of punishment sufficient in itself. In elucidating this rule the Production Code Administration states:

"Suicide as a solution of marital difficulties and immoral entanglements is too easy and too unethical a device. There must be something in the way of right and justice and regeneration to counterbalance it, and, if possible, to outweigh it."

Chapter XXXV

VULGARITY

The Code states that "Vulgarity is the treatment of low, disgusting, unpleasant subjects which decent society considers outlawed from normal conversation," and includes under this heading vulgar expressions and obscene language.

Censorship varies so greatly in the states and communities where it exists that it is impossible to form definite conclusions as to what may or may not be acceptable at any given time. At the present time, most of the censorship action is directed at situations and lines which too definitely picturize or *describe sex situations*; at *crime planning* and execution; and at so-called *double-meaning dialog*. Since all of these must be judged by the context and the manner of delivery, generalizations are of little value.

A survey of censorship reports indicates, however, that the following words have been eliminated in more than one picture by more than one censor board:

Alley-cat (applied to a woman)

Bag (applied to a woman)

Bat (applied to a woman)

Broad (applied to a woman)

Bum (objectionable in England)

Bloody (objectionable in England)

Bronx cheer (the sound)

Chippie

Chink

Cocotte

Courtesan

Dago

Dame
Dump
Eunuch
Fairy (in a vulgar sense)
Fanny
Finger (the)
Filthy
Floozy
Frog (Frenchman)
Goose (When used in vulgar sense)
Goosing (when used in vulgar sense)
Guts
Gigolo (always censored in England)
Greaser
Harlot
"Having a baby"
Hellion
Hellish
Hot (applied to a woman)
Hot mama
House-broken
Hun
Huzzy
"In your hat"
Jeez
Jew
Joint (r e f e r r i n g t o a brothel)
Kike
Louse
Lousy
"Love 'em and leave 'em"

Lover (when meaning illicit sex)
Madame (when relating to prostitution)
Make a pass at
Mating season
Mistress (illicit sex)
Moll
Nance
Nigger
Nerts
Nuts (except when meaning "crazy" as in "You're nuts")
On the make
Pansy
Pooped out
Punk
Razzberry (the sound)
Rump
Sex
Sex appeal
Sexual
Scut
She's nothing more than a—
Sissy (denotes pervert in England)
Slut
Son-of-a
Skirt (referring to a woman)
Spig
Tart

Tom-cat (applied to a man)
Trade (sense of prostitution)
"*Traveling salesman*" and "*F a r m e r's daughter*" jokes
Tramp (applied to a woman)
Trollop
Virtuous (sex inference)
Want you (sex)
Wench
Whore
Wop
Yid

The following represent some of the most commonly deleted subjects, which violate both the Code and censorship rulings:

The "Badger" game
French postcards
Immoral propositions
Kicking or slapping a woman on her posterior
Latch keys (for assignations)
Man and woman in bed together
Nose thumbing, or similar offensive gestures
Strip poker games
Strip-tease
Toilet gags, views of toilets in washrooms; doors marked "Ladies," or "Gentlemen" (even in foreign language); remarks like "I gotta see a man about a dog"; and "When you gotta go, you gotta go." References to bedchambers. Remarks about diapers and wettings.

Chapter XXXVI

FOREIGN NATIONS IN PICTURES

The film involving a foreign villain, or the political activities of foreign nations, is the bane of the industry. Perhaps no other phase of the motion picture industry's work is so little understood and so roundly lambasted as its efforts at diplomacy in the problem of international politics.

The story with a foreign locale, whose main theme is concerned with the romance of the principals, always has the appeal associated with adventuring in far places. It is thoroly welcomed by audiences both here and abroad.

Let the screen story, however, concern itself with social problems, military tactics, or political maneuvers, and immediately trouble begins. Usually the word gets out thru a sort of international grapevine that someone is authoring a movie story before the author himself is conscious of it. The versions that trickle back to Hollywood via the protests of the embassies are usually hair-raising caricatures of the original idea. Many times protests arrive before the author gets his version down on paper.

Unless the political story pays tribute to a foreign nation in some way, Hollywood does not attempt to use an existent political entity. A mythical kingdom is used instead.

In the Fall of 1935, the following item appeared in the New York *World Telegram*:

"Franz Werfel's *Forty Days of Musa Dagh*, which was bought for a picture months before the American translation was out, now has been abandoned. . . . The Turkish government sent out an official communiqué to all friendly nations asking them not to allow the picture to be shown."

Another similar item also appeared in the Madisonville, Ky., *Messenger* of November 5, 1935:

"The movie censors of Spain . . . have just barred . . . 'The Devil is a Woman'. . . The censorship announces that unless the film is withdrawn from world circulation and all copies of it, as well as the original negative, are destroyed, no more of the movies of the company which produced it will be permitted to enter Spain."

The objection to the first-named picture was on political grounds, and of the second-named picture on moral grounds. These instances show conclusively that the American industry cannot afford to ignore the foreign censorship requirements.

In addition, while foreign politics appear to be dear to the heart of many writers, the picture public has proved time and again that it does not want political themes. Historical plots, yes. But modern politics, whether domestic or foreign, no. Political opinions are, probably, too personal and individually divergent to prove a happy choice for pictures. The movie public wants to be entertained; but they have indicated most emphatically that they are not entertained by politics.

The kind souls inspired to write beautiful paeans of peace for the movies feel outraged when their idealistic hopes are "thwarted" by the "awful" producers. The truth of the matter is that if a producer of a large company dared to make a picture denouncing war, his firm would have to pay for his enterprise with their business. So war films will continue to be made which will have to serve as a left-handed plea for peace. One authority on the subject, Guglielmo Ferrero, has said that, actually, the most potent plea for peace is the picture showing the horrors of war. So it seems that the objectives of the idealists and the realists can both be won by the same picture without necessity for controversy on either side.

A story that sky-rocketed to fame because of a front-page battle between the author and the industry was the well-known political novel, *It Can't Happen Here*, by Sinclair Lewis. Representing as it did a caricature of the European conflict transferred to American soil, the story was a potential tinder-box. When the studio, which bought first and thought afterward, realized what it was juggling, and what the total destruction and loss in goodwill and other more tangible assets would amount to, if it were created, the story was shelved. The studio's sigh of relief was heard around the world, and so was Mr. Lewis' denunciation of the industry.

The position of the industry on this and similar type stories is expressed in the commentary on this particular fiasco by the *Motion Picture Herald* of February 22, 1936:

"This week's furore about the sacred cause of freedom and the screen, beginning with a statement from Mr. Sinclair Lewis to the effect that his novel, *It Can't Happen Here,* is being suppressed as motion picture material, will be reverberating around the editorial pages and in the international press for months to come. . . . Mr. Lewis sees Art, Expression, Thought, grabbed by the neck and throttled by a czar. . . . Human rights are crushed under heel. . . .

"There are, however, a number of . . . relevant facts . . . which do not precisely support that view. The motion picture as made in America depends for its prosperity on being international merchandise. There are several foreign markets where Mr. Lewis' novel is not likely to enjoy a very wide circulation. Mr. Lewis can afford, and profitably afford, to write for minorities. The screen has not gone into that business, yet. . . .

"It is probable that Mr. Lewis, and many, many others, do not understand the status of the motion picture, in the eyes, or even minds, of his and our beloved and so infernally democratic public. If a reader of his works, for instance, takes violent exception to the content, that reader is merely annoyed with Mr. Lewis. He is not outraged at Doubleday, Doran & Company, or at the whole art of the printed word. But the motion picture spectator, when he is annoyed, is annoyed with the 'damned movies' and likely as not the theatre where he saw the annoying picture. . . .

"Also Mr. Lewis might try to take the position of an executive trying to operate a business in the face of continuous menace of politicians and those who make instruments of politicians. . . . The motion picture business, it chances, is vulnerable to, and on occasion menaced by, all the governments there are, abroad and at home, including national, state and city legislators. . . .

Mr. Lewis also makes quite a point of observing that there is much propaganda film abroad, pro-Fascist and pro-Communist. That, it must be admitted, has nothing whatever to do with the amusement industry. The films concerned are available in the American market but the picture public, as proven at the box-office, *is not amused thereby.*"

Code Regulations

In dealing with any theme involving foreign nations, or individuals, it is always well to keep in mind the "Good Neighbor" policy. If the writer will try to think of the foreign country about which he is writing in the light of his next-door neighbor from whom he can't move away, and with whom he is in daily contact both in his business and social life, he will not be likely to write into his story anything offensive.

The Code regulations applying to foreign stories read as follows:

"The history, institutions, prominent people and citizenry of other nations shall be represented fairly."

"The just rights, history, and feelings of any nation are entitled to consideration and respectful treatment."

It is, of course, impossible to foretell the problems which any particular story with a foreign flavor will present; and for this reason each story of this type must be judged on its individual merits. The Production Code Administration, thru its representatives, is able to determine the acceptability of a story at any given time by the foreign nations.

A few standard rulings may give some clue as to the problems likely to be encountered with themes dealing with foreign countries or individuals. These are given below.

1. Avoid picturizing in an *unfavorable light* another country's religion, history, institutions, prominent people, and citizenry.

2. Do not write stories suggesting the assassination of prominent people of other countries.

3. Do not portray the characters of the story, if they are villains, as of any specific racial or national type unless you have a sympathetic character in the story of the same nationality.

4. Never raise the question of racial prejudice or racial inferiority.

5. Do not burlesque other nationals.

6. Never use offensive names for other nationals such as:

Hun (German)	Chink (Chinese)
Yid (Jewish)	Greaser (Mexican)
Nigger (Negro)	Dago (Italian)
Frog (Frenchman)	Jap (Japanese)

Since at least 40 per cent of the profit to be made from pictures comes from the exhibition of American films in foreign markets, the importance of observing their regulations is obvious. The major producers are always very careful of their films in which any foreign element appears, and make every effort to cooperate with the Producers' Association for the good-will of the industry in foreign countries.

The rulings given constitute recommendations, as stated above, as part of the industry's good-will program. They are necessarily flexible inasmuch as many factors enter into a story's acceptability which could not be anticipated in advance.

The primary consideration of a story under the Code is that its basic theme conforms to the provisions outlined in the two paragraphs quoted from the Production Code. The details of a story must be judged in the light of its individual plot, and the current political and diplomatic status.

Foreign Censorship

A survey of the foreign censorship requirements, as given in the 1936 issue of the *Film Daily Year Book*, provides an interesting and comprehensive view of the various national attitudes.

General censorship on moral, political and religious grounds is very strict in Albania, Australia, Bolivia, Czechoslovakia, Egypt, El Salvador, England, Estonia, Finland, India, Lithuania, Norway, Palestine, Peru, Soviet Russia and Turkey. In the Dominican Republic, objections are raised most frequently on moral grounds; the same is true of Nicaragua; in East Africa there is a particularly rigid censorship on gangster films; Greece prohibits any communistic propaganda; Spain concerns itself with both moral and political aspects, and provides for the withdrawal of films upon protest from the foreign embassies; Yugoslavia also has a strict censorship on political subjects; while the rest of the world practices a more or less rigid censorship on some or all of these points.

The Film Daily Year Book lists the specific requirements of the countries indicated below, as follows:

Argentina

The types of pictures unacceptable for exhibition in Argentina are those: offensive to the morals or established customs of a country. Pictures of insane institutions and hospitals; films which ridicule religious subjects and beliefs; and films of a political character which might encourage disputation and trouble.

Bahamas

No ganster films are permitted to be shown. A film law forbids the presentation of any film of a treasonable, seditious, profane, blasphemous, immoral, indecent or obscene character.

Barbados

Censorship, such as it is, is quite strict. Excessive sex emphasis, and cruelty to persons as represented in the gangster films are considered objectionable.

Brazil

The following are set forth as reasons for the whole or partial rejection of a picture by the Board of Censors: (1) offense to public decency; (2) suggestive of crime; (3) conveying illusions which might prove prejudicial to international relations; (4) insulting to race, collective groups or religious sects; (5) offensive to National dignity or provocative of defiance to public order.

British Malaya

The types of films banned most frequently have been gangster films and films connected with gun play, films depicting racial love scenes, and films in which the criminal element is predominant. There appears to be a definite inclination on the part of representatives of certain religious groups, particularly the Mohammedans, to impress their views on the authorities in respect of pictures belittling in any way the Mohammedan character or faith. The cleanup campaign in the American film industry has been instrumental in the smaller number of films banned this year.

Bulgaria

The most important factors in determining the acceptance of a film are the following: (1) the film must contain nothing dangerous to the State (communistic or anarchistic propaganda); (2) immoral subjects and pictures are not allowed; (3) anything offensive to the Royal House, to the Army and to any country with diplomatic relations with Bulgaria, would not be permitted.

China

Stories that alluringly depict the younger Chinese generation frequenting night clubs and indulging in other similar foreign pastimes are frowned upon unless strong moral is included showing the undesirable effects of such living. Scenarios showing the advantages of simple living, of thrift and unselfish service to family and country, of nationalism and the dignity of labor, these are a few of the subjects favored by the authorities as suitable for screen material.

Costa Rica

Films are censored by the Government if complaint is made by some religious or other agency.

Denmark

At a recent conference at Oslo, Norway, attended by the film censors of three Scandinavian countries, a resolution was adopted to the effect that censorship of gangster and so-called horror films, as well as wild-west films depicting criminal characters and approaching gangster films in type, should be more rigid in the future.

Germany

In order to meet the demands of the Nazi code of morals, censorship was rendered considerably sharper in practice. The apparent severity of the censorship policy would indicate a market supply of domestic films of distinct National character.

Haiti

The Department of the Interior is given the power to censor films which are considered to be immoral or dangerous to the maintenance of internal order.

Hungary

Pictures are censored by the official board solely with regard to public morals and the safety of the State.

Italy

Censorship continues to be rigorous, though not unreasonable. But even after a film has passed the censors and been screened, it can be objected to by any private citizen or organization, on complaint to the

police, who have the power to review the film and, if
deemed necessary or advisable, to order it off the screen.

Jamaica

Six pictures refused in 1934 were of the underworld
type or were suggestive from a moral view. Pictures
showing drunkenness or unconventional frivolity on the
part of the white people will not pass the censor. This
is because of the large Negro population. Pictures
showing robberies and holdups are banned, since it is
believed that they might have a bad impresson on some
of the lower classes and might act as an incentive to
crime.

Japan

Censorship is fairly lenient, but definitely objectionable scenes dealing with riots, sedition, revolution and
so-called "Red" propaganda are deleted.

Mexico

The censors are particularly interested in securing
the use of correct Spanish and eliminating scenes which
are termed too hot or which may be derogatory to
Mexico.

Netherlands

Censorship is quite strict, barring films (or parts
thereof) which are deemed apt to incite disorder or
immorality or which have a certain (political) tendency.
Catholic censorship is exercised over all films.

Netherland India

Censorship is strict as to all problems dealing with
racial differences, sex, mob scenes and the use of fire

arms, but more lenient than in certain other Asiatic countries.

New Zealand

A film law provides that the approval of the Censor shall not be given with respect to any films which, in his opinion, depict any matter that is contrary to public order or decency.

Rumania

Bad films are considered those which by their way of showing life are likely to "pervert the soul," and to constitute propaganda for actions harming public welfare. Such are films representing: criminal actions, constituting a school of crime or infringement of the law; political actions against public and social safety in which hostility is shown between two categories of citizens, or which might be a suggestion for non-submission to laws; films affecting the dignity or honor of this country or of other countries, or encouraging hatred and hostility among people; films which might diminish faith of a country in itself, in its leaders and the respect due to these; films mocking or detracting from respect towards fundamental institutions of the State: Church, Army, School; films showing scenes of debauchery and vice, which constitute an assault against the respect for moral purity of the youth and the family; films which through violence or barbarism might produce nervous shocks in the spectators. Films containing scenes of the kind mentioned do not change their character by the fact that the end may be considered as moral.

South Africa

Censorship still remains most stringent. There has been some agitation regarding the Church-Censorship

Movement and various societies have formed themselves into Vigilant Committees to check up on the type of film shown.

Sweden

As a rule films showing suicides, terrifying scenes of other crimes contrary to general law and morals, as well as acting that may have a bad influence are forbidden. Films in which murders, robberies, holdups, gangster life, etc., appear, fall in the "children prohibited" class.

Syria

A commission previews the films, censoring them as to morals, public security, respect to religions and races, and political propaganda.

Trinidad

Films are rejected or deleted for the following reasons: Predominance of criminal acts; scenes offensive to national and racial sentiment; mutiny; murders; shooting scenes; bedroom scenes; vulgar dialogue; horror themes and scenes; and realistic scenes of torture.

Venezuela

As a rule censorship is not so strict where morality is concerned, but definitely so regarding revolutionary or anti-government propaganda.

SCREEN WRITING PROBLEMS

Chapter XXXVII

THE DEMAND FOR A NEW TYPE
OF SCREEN WRITER

This study would be incomplete if it did not touch upon one important phase of the motion picture industry's problem resulting directly from the Decency Drive. That is the demand for a new type of screen writer.

There are two centres of sophistication in the United States—New York and Hollywood. To them come a select group of the intellectuals, the intelligentsia and the restless spirits who intend to make writing their life work. The very fact that so often these people gather together, form cliques and have few if any other contacts tends to isolate them from the popular thought of the moment.

As a result they too often forget that in the three thousand miles between New York and Hollywood are over 120 million people who are living normal lives and who subscribe to the conservative forms of behavior. Of the vast motion picture audience, sometimes estimated at 85 million per week, it is undoubtedly true that practically all of these people patronize the motion picture theatres as an "escape" from their somewhat monotonous daily routine. They receive a definite vicarious thrill from the pictures which are presented to them. In view of this it is obvious that, in order to be successful, the thoughts and actions of their favorite players must conform to *their* ideas of what is fit and proper so that they may sympathize whole-heartedly and enter into the spirit of the picture which they are witnessing. A picture which fails to meet these requirements in its theme and its development, may be acclaimed as "art" or as "a daring new departure" by the critics, but experience has long demonstrated that such pictures fail miserably in their popular appeal.

Since the enforcement of the Production Code in 1934, embodying the conservative principles of conduct, this situation has become aggravated. Today the motion picture industry is faced with a scarcity of "acceptable" stories.

One of the requirements of the new screen writer is an understanding of the standard of behavior subscribed to by our average communities. Where is this new screen writer to come from? The obvious answer is—from the "average community." But there are definite prerequisites for screen writing—talent, education, and preparation. The subsequent chapters will suggest how these prerequisites may be met, and how such a writer may prepare himself for screen writing.

Chapter XXXVIII

COMMON MISCONCEPTIONS ABOUT SCREEN WRITING

It is necessary before proceeding further to clear up a number of common misconceptions on the subject of screen writing.

The first of these is: *continuity form is not essential.* Every new writer seems to labor under the delusion that he cannot write for the screen until he learns how to write his story in continuity form, or else gets someone to put it in such form for him.

Perhaps this was true in the old days, before the talkies came into being, when camera angles were confined to closeups and long shots. It was no task to write a continuity scenario in those days—you put the action on one side of the page and the dialog on the other side, and that was all there was to it. Today conditions are different.

Each studio has its own staff of technical writers. A staff writer usually prepares a treatment from the original story material; then the dialog is added by someone specializing in that work. After the dialog is approved by the production head a continuity writer is assigned to make a blueprint of the production, suggesting camera angles, close-ups, medium shots, long shots and novel photographic effects. He also arranges the scenes according to number. The talking pictures have made necessary three times the number of writers required for the silent pictures, and it is three times as difficult to prepare a talking picture continuity as it was a silent picture script!

It is a waste of time for the writer, whether an amateur or a professional, to prepare a continuity scenario of his screen story. The studios prepare their own continuity scenarios to fit the individual requirements. Further, a more simple form is likely to obtain a quicker reading by the studio story editor than a lengthy scenario of this type.

The second very important fact to remember is that *it is not necessary to come to Hollywood* in order to find an opportunity to write for the movies. Life's minor tragedies occur when, following the enthusiastic praise of friends, the would-be writer comes to Hollywood to "crash the studios" with the entire hopes, and often finances, of the family bound up in a "scenario."

A few years ago studios were willing to read stories from amateur writers. And they did read thousands. The results were discouraging. As a number of the studios reported:

"We absolutely refuse to accept stories submitted by unknown writers; and discourage even known writers from sending in stories unless we have solicited them. The reason for this is that we have found from past experience that there will be only one good story in several thousand, and the percentage of material obtainable in this manner does not offset the expense of reading the many manuscripts."

Another reason for refusing manuscripts sent in by unknown persons is to avoid subsequent claims for plagiarism. Consequently no stories mailed in to the studios are even opened, but the envelope is stamped "Refused" and returned to the writer. In the words of a studio which had this experience, "We refuse to accept stories from unknown writers for reading, owing to the ridiculous claims of plagiarism they make afterwards if we do not buy."

Therefore the studios have been forced, in self-protection, to adopt the stringent and inflexible rule never to read scenarios or stories from unknown writers, or even to interview, or discuss the story with the writer.

Today the studio gates are guarded, and no one goes in without a pass—not even the officials can get by without the approval of the guards. Telephone calls to the story editor, or to any one else, avail the writer nothing, as studios make it a practice never to deal with writers except thru agents. A letter for an interview will bring a refusal. If the scenario is mailed in, it will be returned unopened. There isn't a loophole anywhere.

If the writer then makes the rounds' to see the "friends" of the enthusiastic friend back home who urged him to come to Hollywood, he will find that no outsider has any influence in opening the studio doors to an unknown writer. Not even those with studio connections would risk suggesting such a possibility to studio officials.

The only chance for the unknown author—or for any known writer—is the reputable *agent*. Thru him any good story may find a reading for studio production, and the stay-at-home has as good a chance as the writer who goes to Hollywood to chase the will-of-the-wisp, success.

In the encouraging words of the *Hollywood Reporter*, of June 23, 1936:

"Studio executives are evincing a continued partiality toward original yarns from recognized writers, *and even giving consideration to unknowns sponsored by reliable agents.*"

Writing for the screen is not as easy as some people seem to believe, however. There are definite requirements, and educational qualifications. Before thinking of means of disposing of a story, the writer should first determine whether he is qualified to write a story for screen dramatization.

CHAPTER XXXIX

EDUCATIONAL PREREQUISITES FOR LITERARY WORK

While there is a wide class of people who *get* ideas about writing, actually there are only two types of individuals who ever *do* anything about it. As indicated in the following comment, these are the writers with "literary" training; and those within the "non-literary" category, having little or no training for writing. Of the two, the former needs to be encouraged to write more; and the latter needs to be trained to write better. The consensus of opinion from the studios is that:

"There seems to be an oversupply of stories from non-literary people—*and an undersupply from literary people.*"

Literary People

It might be well, at the outset, to define what we mean by the "literary" class, for this is the only class qualified to attempt screen writing. The writer must be able to fulfill these requirements:

a) The first—and foremost—is imagination, essential to the concept and development of ideas;

b) The second is the literary ability and dramatic skill to develop the story from the standpoint of plot and characterization;

c) The third is the ability to express the ideas on paper.

Broadly speaking, the individual who can fulfill these three essentials by virtue of education, training or experience is classifiable as a "literary" person.

The individual who has properly educated himself for this type of work is, of course, the one who has taken his academic studies with writing as his goal, with majors in English, dramatic arts, journalism, or publicity and advertising.

The man who is trained for some professional work such as law, medicine, science, or engineering, by virtue of his broad educational background and daily contact with people, often finds himself well equipped to undertake writing. This individual, too, is classifiable as a "literary" person.

The professional writer—by which term we mean the writer who has succeeded in having his material published *in a medium of national circulation*—the author of a novel, a short story, a play, or a biography is unquestionably qualified to undertake screen writing with a better than average chance of success. This is the professional "literary" class with writing successes to its credit as distinguished from the amateur "literary" class which has the proper training or background but lacks experience.

The Non-Literary Person

The non-literary class comprises, of course, all amateur writers having little or no literary training or educational background. The greatest difficulty encountered by the non-literary person is his inability—even where he may have a good idea—to express himself on paper. Too often he finds himself incapable, as well, of developing a properly balanced plot from his basic idea.

Before attempting to write anything at all, therefore, he should prepare himself to meet the second and third requirements, and thus to qualify for the "literary" classification. It is assumed, of course, that the individual undertaking such study has imagination, for that is the prime requisite for any type of writing.

The following courses, as indicated, may be taken in evening high school classes given for adults; in University extension divisions; or, if neither is convenient, they can be taken thru the University correspondence courses.

Evening High Schools

High School grammar and composition
Literature and reading courses
Short story writing, and story markets

University Extension Classes

All advanced writing courses
History and technique of drama
Great personalities and similar history courses

University Correspondence Courses

The person desiring to write, should refer to his nearest first class college or university and choose the same types of courses as those suggested above.

No one should attempt writing unless he has a thoro knowledge of grammar and composition. He should also study writing forms, so that he will understand the principles of motivation, character delineation, and plot development. Without an understanding of these basic principles the writer will *not* be successful in his attempts at screen dramatization.

The writer should fulfill at least the High School program outlined. If he can also undertake the University subjects, his opportunities will naturally be greater.

Chapter XL

THE STORY IDEA

The Origin of the Idea

The idea for a screen story may be suggested by any number of things. One may get an idea from a real life incident; from current events; from a newspaper story; from a court trial; from the business, domestic, or social affairs of one's every-day life; in fact, from an infinite variety of sources.

Having an idea, however, one should analyze it to determine whether it is sufficiently good, new, or novel to develop into the theme which it suggests. The studios are not looking merely for stories—they are looking for new *ideas, adaptable* to the screen. Out of several hundred stories there may be only a few really good ideas—and only one or two which might lend themselves to screen dramatization. The writer should bear in mind that the studios have no lack of trite and banal material. His story must treat some new and unusual phase of life, or have some novel twist that takes it out of the category of the commonplace. The ability to judge this point is necessarily gained only by a study of dramatic values and presupposes an adequate educational background. The *Hollywood Reporter* of June 23, 1936 states:

"The greatest boom in original story sales since early film days is currently hitting a peak. . . . In line with the trend to originals is the policy . . . of buying magazine short stories *for a dramatic twist or idea,* then assigning staff writers to concoct a virtual original around it."

The amateur writer errs most often on this crucial point—he never stops to analyze his idea. The tendency to go right ahead and write a story about anything that pops into his mind accounts for the facts that rarely more than one, out of a thousand stories from amateurs, has an idea either new, or worth while developing at all. In order to save much wasted effort, therefore, the writer should analyze his ideas before he spends any labor on them.

Is the idea acceptable under the code?

Having decided upon the theme which the idea suggests, the writer should refer to the analysis of the Production Code given in the previous section to determine whether the theme can be treated for the screen. The Code regulations will also be found in the Appendix.

The writer should bear in mind that his theme and plot must conform to all the regulations governing it under the Code. For instance, if the theme is based on the "triangle," reference should first be made to the chapter dealing with this specific subject. Second, since the story deals with a sex problem, it must also conform to the general Code regulations applying to "Sex in general." If, in addition to this basic theme, an element of murder, let us say, is introduced, the crime regulations specifically outlined for "Murder" would have to be met, as well as the General Regulations relating to crime and dealing with the treatment of law-enforcing agencies and individuals in screen stories.

The chief concern, from the writer's standpoint, is to make the *basic* story acceptable under the Code. The *details* of plot and dialog need not be subjected to such close scrutiny inasmuch as any studio considering the story for purchase would take care of these details. Frequently, too, many changes are made by the studio to bring the story within individual and unpredictable requirements. Only the basic theme therefore is seriously analyzed by the studios for its screen adaptability and acceptibility.

Another important point for the writer to remember is that the final responsibility for Code conformity lies with the studio. Under the arrangements which the motion picture producers have with the Producers' Association, all studios, whether belonging to the major or independent groups, members and non-members alike, have the privilege of sending in stories in any and all forms to the Production Code Administration for reading and detailed analysis. Where necessary the Code office offers definite suggestions for changing the story, plot, dialog and action to bring it into conformity with the Code. Many lengthy conferences are held with the studio officials and the studio writing staff to the end that stories may be made thoroly acceptable.

The Production Code Administration has the responsibility, not only of reading the original story, novel, play, biography, synopsis, or original, but of reading the scenarios made from these and every line of dialog and action which is thereafter amended or added; and of reviewing the film to determine the reactions to be gained from seeing and hearing the drama on the screen. Only after the film itself has been found acceptable is a certificate of approval granted to the studio, with the right to employ the symbol of the Production Code Administration and the certificate number on the title card of the picture.

The services of the Production Code Administration *are restricted to producers and to studios.* They are not available to any outsiders; or to writers or their literary agents. A story must be submitted to the Code office by the studio itself—it will not be accepted from any other source. The Production Code Administration encourages producers to send stories to them for analysis *before purchase*. This is to prevent the monetary loss inevitably accruing in cases where stories are purchased and later prove to be *basically unacceptable* under the Code. Most studios do so at present.

How can a story be developed from the idea?

The writer must concern himself with three major elements in writing or adapting any stories for the screen. These are:

1. The love story;
2. The conflict;
3. The action.

The prime requisite for a good screen story is *action*. Therefore, before a story is written in its final form, it should be synopsized with emphasis on that part of the story which indicates the *action* which may be photographed. With this emphasis in mind, the writer will be less tempted to resort to lengthy dialog or subtle psychological situations which are so difficult to portray on the screen without boring the audience.

If the writer is adapting a story for the screen, he will do well to use the supplementary synopsis form to develop the screen story rather than to attempt to rewrite the original story. In that way, he will be writing for both the literary market and for the screen market. When the writer's original story (a novel, short story, play, or biography) is presented to the studio, it can be indicated that the supplementary synopsis suggests the *screen* story which can be developed from it. With both the original story and the screen synopsis at hand, the

studio editor has the opportunity of deciding for himself
what screen possibilities are inherent in the writer's story,
aside from those suggested in the writer's screen synopsis
of his original story.

The Love Story

By the curious formula which is generally accepted in
Hollywood, most stories adapted for the screen must
have a so-called "love" story. Even where the original
story does not have a strong love interest, this element
should be introduced for the screen version. This does
not mean that the hero must necessarily be a party to the
love affair; but some one of the important characters
supporting the principal should, if the love interest is not
consistent with the hero's characterization, be shown in
the emotional role. Naturally where such love interest is
introduced, it must be knitted into the plot in such a way
as to support it, and to become a motivating factor. It
should not be a parallel or unrelated incident.

The Conflict

Inasmuch as the conflict is the most important part of
the plot providing most of the action, suspense and
drama leading directly up to the climax, this element
should be strongly emphasized in all screen stories. A
story with a strong conflict, or a series of conflicts, is one
ideally suited for screen dramatization.

The Action

Wherever possible action should be introduced instead
of dialog. Have the characters moving about, doing
things, going places instead of sitting around talking.
Show things *happening*. Make the plot revolve around
incidents rather than around talk. Inject this supple-

mentary action into the story in such a way that it becomes part of the plot motivation and leads naturally and consistently into the high-lighted, dramatic action provided by the conflict. Action should be used as the prelude, interlude and postlude to climaxes. In other words, whenever a character can be made to express a story point by movement, either in lieu of, or as a dramatic aid to dialog, use action. *Dialog should be used only to explain action, never to express it.*

The habit of action-thinking can be developed by actual practice, as suggested in the chapter "Experiments in Screen Writing"—by synopsizing books from which current motion pictures are made, and comparing results when the picture is released for exhibition. A few months of such training will help establish the proper mental mood for screen writing; and, at the same time, add a fillip to the writer's other literary efforts. The most relaxing type of fiction and the most popular kind is that which literally jumps from verb to verb. An analysis of the fiction of bygone days that has outlived its age will reveal a veritable storehouse of exciting thrillers. That is a factor which accounts for the amazing success in adapting the "classics" to the screen. The stories of "Quo Vadis," "Tale of Two Cities," "David Copperfield," "Captain Blood," "Count of Monte Cristo," "Les Miserables," to mention but a few outstanding screen successes, were packed with *action*.

Stories suggesting action have greater opportunities for sale. Therefore the writer interested in the screen market should emphasize this element in writing or adapting stories for screen presentation.

CHAPTER XLI

FORMS USED IN SCREEN WRITING

Since it is necessary for the writer (except in rare cases) to prove his literary ability by evidence of a published short story, novel, book, play or biography, before a literary agent will undertake to represent him, it is obvious that he must be familiar with one or all of these forms of writing before he can even *think* of screen writing. Therefore the question of "form" is to be decided by the writer's own preference and experience. The professional writer, in writing *direct* for the screen, would find it an economy of time and effort to use the "original" form.

The Continuity

As stated elsewhere, no writer should attempt to write a continuity unless specifically requested to do so by the studio itself. First of all, it is useless to the studio unless it is written under their supervision for a specific star and specific requirements. Second, the scenario form is the most difficult form to read; and as the readability of a story contributes much to its sales value, this form is a distinct hindrance.

The Short Story

Within certain limits, the short story is a good form, provided it does not follow the mechanics of the "incident" type. If the short story form is used, it must be a *complete* story, with good build-up, rise, cumulative climax, and rapid fall.   It should actually be a short novel.   The advantages of the short story form are its brevity, readability and clarity.

The Novel

The novel, like the short story, is also good screen form, whether in typed form, published in a magazine, or in book form.   However, a synopsis should always accompany the novel to facilitate reading.   This is suggested because the length of a novel is usually such that it takes considerable time to read it.   If the synopsis indicates an interesting story, the novel is more likely to be read, than if the novel is submitted without the outline of the story.

The Play

Because of the obvious limitations of the legitimate stage, and the conformity of the play to these limits, the play form is not entirely desirable for submission to studios.   It is difficult—and takes time and imagination— to transfer the drama mentally from the stage to the screen.   The stage depends largely on dialog; the screen depends almost wholly on action.   The story editor has not the time for mental gymnastics; consequently the screen possibilities in a play may remain submerged under its dialog and the story be rejected as unsuitable. The only alternative the playwright has, to assure a reading of his play, is to send with it a synopsis outlining the *screen action* and possibilities inherent in his play.

This does not apply, of course, in the case of a produced play which has had a successful run, and has been audience-tested.   Such a play has gained prestige.   Its possibilities are more easily visualized, too, when presented on the stage where the emotional appeal of the actors is a great contributing factor. The produced play is naturally the easiest to sell.

The Biography

The biography form is not employed to a great extent as a source for screen material. Within the past year but three biographies provided the basis for a screen play. However, the writer who has written a biography which he believes has screen possibilities would increase his chances if he submits a synopsis with it outlining and emphasizing the screen action and possibilities.

The "Original"

The "original" is exactly what its name implies—an original story, written especially for the screen. Its form is very simple. It is merely a narrative, in present tense, spotted with dialog, giving the story in the form of sequences or chapters. It differs from the synopsis in that it takes the narrative step by step from its beginning to its end, instead of summarizing the climax of the story and then highlighting, thru a series of back-tracks, its plot development. In the "original" form the plot *unfolds* itself; in the synopsis the plot is explained in the light of the climax.

The only dialog necessary in the "original" is that required to indicate the trend of the story, or to delineate character. It is, as is evident, but an exposition of the action and characterization, and serves as an excellent medium for screen writing since it speaks in the terms of the screen itself—action. It is easy to visualize the development of the screen play from this form.

The "original" may run anywhere from eight pages to fifty pages or more depending upon the volubility of the writer. Where it is lengthy, it is well to supplement this form with an explanatory synopsis for quick reading and analysis.

The Synopsis

The synopsis, as stated above, is a short form, which might be used either to supplement other forms or as a form sufficient in itself. If it is used alone, it should be amplified to include the important details of plot and dialog indicating the trend and action.

The synopsis is usually preceded by a short summary indicating in a few well-chosen words the theme of the story. This is followed by the synopsis which gives, first, the climax, and proceeds from that point to introduce the elements and factors building up to the climax and contributing to the denoument.

Synopses may run anywhere from a single page to ten or more pages depending upon the number of significant details requiring amplification.

It is usually better, of course, to use the synopsis in short form to supplement other forms, since the synopsis, because of its peculiar form, limits the exposition of the story to some extent. In the majority of cases, the "original" form is to be preferred in place of a lengthy synopsis because its exposition is more closely allied to the actual film form and, consequently, its screen dramatization is more easily visualized by the reader.

Chapter XLII

REGISTRATION AND COPYRIGHTING
OF STORY MATERIAL

Registration

Stories intended for the screen may be registered with the Screen Writers' Guild of the Authors' League of America, 1655 North Cherokee Street, Hollywood, Calif.; and with the Authors' League of America, 9 East 38th Street, New York City.

The purpose of such registration is to give the author *proof* of the priority of his work over any pirated version. Each manuscript received by the Guild is stamped with a registration number, date and time of receipt, and is filed. An entry is then made in the Guild records. *Evidence* is thus provided for as to the date when the author had the complete work in his possession. The charge for such registration is $1 to non-members and 50 cents to members.

Neither the Screen Writers' Guild, nor the Authors' League of America is concerned with the sale of manuscripts. They have no facilities for the handling, sale of, or submission of material to agents or studios. Their only function is to register story material for the purpose outlined.

Copyrighting

Full and complete copyright information and application blanks can be had free of charge by writing to the

Copyright Office of the United States, Library of Congress, Washington, D.C.

Under the copyright laws at present in effect, only *published* works can be copyrighted. No provision is made for the copyrighting of literary works in advance of publication. Therefore *manuscripts* of novels, short stories, motion picture scenarios or any other literary work should *not* be sent to the Copyright Office before they are published—or they should not be sent at all if they are not to be published. The Copyright Office Bulletin states that "they are protected under the *common law* against unauthorized use in whole or in part up to the time of actual publication, and no legal purpose is served by sending such manuscripts to the Copyright Office." This refers, of course, to literary works being prepared for publication. Unpublished *dramatic* works, and unpublished musical works may be copyrighted. Motion picture stories do *not* come under the classification of "dramatic works."

It is evident that the writer who does not publish his story must protect it in some other way than by copyright, and it is in this connection that the service of the Screen Writers' Guild and the Authors' League of America becomes of value, since it provides him with full proof and evidence of the priority of his works over subsequent versions. Almost all of the screen writers in Hollywood and New York take advantage of these registration services.

Published Works

All published material, bearing the copyright of the author or the publisher is sufficiently protected by the copyright to dispense with the registration of such works. However, if the published work is to be sent to agents or studios accompanied by a synopsis or other treatment indicating the screen adaptation of the published work—particularly if the adaptation differs radically from the original in any important detail—then the supplementary form should be registered with the Screen Writers' Guild or the Authors' League to protect the screen version of the story.

Adaptations of Other Literary Works

No writer should attempt to adapt a published and copyrighted work, which is not his own, for screen dramatization without securing the permission of the publisher. To write a screen version of a published, copyrighted work without permission from the copyright owner would amount to plagiarism.

Published works on which the copyright has elapsed are, of course, in the public domain and free to anyone. But the writer should make certain of this fact before proceeding to adapt the material.

Copies Required

The writer should make three copies of his manuscript—the original to be sent to the agent or studio; the second copy to be registered with the Screen Writers' Guild or the Authors' League of America; and the third copy for his own files. The writer should always have one copy of his manuscript for his own reference; occasionally manuscripts go astray and if the author does not have a copy of his story, the loss is a serious one for he may not be able to rewrite the material in its original form.

CHAPTER XLIII

WHAT PROTECTION DOES COPYRIGHT AFFORD?

Just how much of a story is copyrightable? What is plagiarism? The answers to these two questions are given by the Court rulings which have clarified and simplified the determination of what constitutes plagiarism. The Supreme Court decision is of particular interest in that it provides an excellent precedent upon which to base judgment. The following record of plagiarism suits appeared in one of the trade journals of the motion picture industry which is issued annually—*The Film Daily Year Book (of 1935)*—and to which reference can be made for information on current verdicts:

"An authoress sued to enjoin presentation, production, distribution or exhibition of the play entitled 'Death Takes a Holiday' claiming it was plagiarism of one she had previously written. Both plays were annexed to her complaint. The Court read and compared both plays, found no plagiarism and dismissed the complaint.

"Comment: The Court held, (1) a claim of copyright infringement based on plagiarism should be determined by a reading and comparison of the plays themselves by the Court without the necessity of any trial (similarities and differences can be fully presented by way of oral arguments and briefs) ; (2) *the test of plagiarism is simple. The plagiarism must be something which* ORDINARY OBSERVATION *would recognize as having been taken from the work of another* AND NOT BY FINE ANALYSIS OR DISSECTION BY AN EXPERT; (3) the exact text need not be followed for plagiarism and piracy may consist of appropriating the action of a play without any of the words, *but a plot or mere concept of a situation around which to build and develop literary and artistic adornment is not copyrightable.*

"This case is of interest because of the clean cut rules which it enunciates for testing plagiarism and also because the author appealed to the United States Circuit Court of Appeals and to the United States Supreme Court but the instant court's decision was not reversed."

In the case cited above, by that amazing coincidence apparent in both the literary and inventive field, both parties had conceived a very similar and unusual idea; but each had developed the idea in a different way. One of these stories was made into a motion picture; and thus came to the attention of the other writer who naturally assumed—as most writers do—that nobody else could possibly have had the same idea. Since the idea was a very unusual one, it is not to be wondered at that the author took the case to Court. In so doing, she has helped other writers; for the precedent established by the United States Supreme Court makes it plain that, no matter how original, unusual, startling, or weird an idea a writer may have, he has no monopoly on *ideas,* and, therefore, no basis for a plagiarism suit if several other writers chance to have the same idea. It is an amazing fact, substantiated by numerous records of such cases, that one person is rarely ever the exclusive possessor of a new idea—inventive devices almost invariably come into the Patent Office in twos and threes, and almost all at the same time (usually within several days or weeks after the receipt of the first application). Whether ideas, once conceived are "catching" and so transmitted to other minds, or whether they are universally present and ready to be conceived by any fertile minds which may contact this mental stratosphere, the fact remains that if the writer has an "original" idea, the chances are 99 to 1 that at least three other people have the same idea at the same time.

The point, then, which determines plagiarism, is not the *idea*, or "concept of a situation" around which the plot is built and developed; but the action and dialog, location of scenes, etc., which the situation inspires and motivates. Even with as banal a situation as a triangle, it is obvious that one cannot sue every other writer for thinking of a triangle on which to base his story. Each writer, starting from his particular premise, idea, or concept of a situation, is free to develop that situation along dramatic lines peculiarly his own. On the other hand, if the action and the details of development of his story were exactly the same as another's, and were based on the same idea, the question of plagiarism might arise to be determined. The chances for such a thing happening are very small, for while more than one writer may get the same idea at the same time, the background, training, environment, mental outlook, and other personal factors would color the different stories, and affect their development in such a way as to mark each one with the stamp of the particular individual writing them.

Another interesting suit is recorded in the *Film Daily Year Book of 1936*, which further analyzes the test of plagiarism, and specifically identifies the elements of the story which are copyrightable:

"An. author sued Paramount claiming that the photoplay 'Blonde Venus' infringed the copyright of his play. The author had copyrighted the play in 1931. He thereafter submitted it to the producer who produced and distributed 'Blonde Venus' in 1932.

"The producer denied plagiarism and alleged that 'the play and the basic plot, theme, ideas, sequences, events, and episodes in the plaintiff's work are not novel or original with the plaintiff but constitute common property residing in the public domain and are not properly the subject of copyright under the copyright laws of the United States.'

"By stipulation the play and the photoplay were attached to the bill to permit the court to examine and decide from them whether the producer had copied the play.

"The Court dismissed the complaint. He said:

" 'If it appears from the examination of the play and the photoplay that the photoplay does not infringe, there is no reason for having a trial. . .' From the synopsis of the play and the photoplay, it is evident that while both authors make use of a common fundamental plot, the stories told are not the same. There is a material difference in the characters of the principals and the episodes, although there is bound to be a resemblance in the basic narrative. The scenes, locale, and action differ. The dialogue also is materially different and naturally the stories are not the same. . . . There was no infringement of the complainant's copyright.'

"*Comment*: The Court said, 'It is true that an author has an exclusive right to his own treatment of an idea, subject or plot. . . . The Copyright law protects the means of *expressing* an idea; . . . if the same idea can be expressed in a plurality of totally different manners, a plurality of copyrights may result, and no infringement will exist.'

"The Court recognized the producer's access to the play and the likelihood that some of the ideas found in the defendants' photoplay were suggested by the complainant's play and other older books and plays.

"He decided, however, that 'defendants have taken nothing from any of them that was not in the public domain or public property.' "

Published works on which the copyright has expired, and public records of current events are generally considered to be in the "public domain." According to the Court rulings on the two cases cited, it appears that basic story ideas are also in the "public domain" and hence are not copyrightable.

Consequently, the idea on which the story is based, and any part of the story which is taken from material within the "public domain" is not copyrightable. Whatever additional action and dialog is included in the play, exclusive of the material taken from the "public

domain" is protected by the copyright law. The author
who bases his story on material in the "public domain,"
however, cannot claim infringement of copyright unless
the *entire* play is lifted, including the part he has himself
contributed to it.

To establish the Court's decision on this point, another case recorded in the *Film Daily Year Book of 1935*
is quoted having reference to material adapted from the
"public domain":

"The plaintiff wrote a play based upon a famous murder
trial. Someone else later wrote a novel based upon the same
trial which was, however, her own work and not an infringement of the plaintiff's play. The plaintiff's play was offered to
a producer who submitted it to the Hays' Office. The latter refused its censorship okay and the matter of selling the play was
dropped.

"Thereafter the producer bought the novel and made a picture thereon. Plaintiff sued for infringement of copyright.

"The U. S. District Court held in the producer's favor.

"Comment: The Court said:

"(1) The basic plot of the trial itself *was in the public
domain and not included in the copyright of the play*
which it had inspired.

"(2) Unless the entire play was lifted, no relief would be
granted.

"(3) *Ideas are not copyrightable.*"

All of these decisions establish the point that whether
the idea upon which a story is based is an original concept; or suggested by some incident in the public records,
or other uncopyrightable sources, the copyright which he
obtains for his story does not include the monopoly of
the source material, but only the development and treatment of the idea. These rulings are entirely logical, for
while basic plot ideas are few, there is an infinite variety
of treatment and development.

CHAPTER XLIV

LEGITIMATE CHANNELS FOR MARKETING THE SCREEN STORY

The literary agent provides the best—and, in most cases, the only—source of studio contact possible to the writer. The only alternative contact is provided thru the publisher of the writer's works.

Publishers, particularly the larger ones, make it a practice to send regularly galley proofs of new novels to the story editors of the various studios. In addition, the Story Departments of the studios read current literature to discover new ideas. As a result of this, an author of published material may receive an offer for the screen rights to his story.

The Importance of the Literary Agent

The studios prefer to deal with writers thru literary agents because these agents understand their needs and methods, and provide a quick channel of contact and information.

From the standpoint of the writer, it is usually to his advantage to have a representative who can discuss terms and take care of business details with which the writer may not be sufficiently familiar to bargain to his own advantage. Consequently even writers who have direct studio connections usually have literary agents to represent their interests and to handle all business matters.

The names of literary agents may be secured by writing to the Hollywood Chamber of Commerce, Hollywood, Calif.; the Los Angeles Better Business Bureau, Los Angeles, Calif.; the New York Chamber of Commerce, New York City, or by referring to the *Film Daily Year Book,* published annually by the Film Daily, 6425 Hollywood Blvd., Hollywood, Calif.; or the *International Motion Picture Almanac,* published every year by the Quigley Publishing Company, Rockefeller Center, New York City. The names and addresses of the various studios are also given in these publications, with a list of their personnel both in Hollywood and New York. Most public libraries carry copies of these two official publications of the industry.

The names of a number of agents, who may be communicated with by mail, are also given in the Appendix, for the benefit of those who do not have access to the reference books mentioned above.

Choosing the Agent

A knowledge of the operating methods of legitimate agents will be helpful to the writer in selecting the right representative. There are both large and small agencies in Hollywood and New York.

The larger agencies have very exacting requirements. They accept screen material only from writers who have established names in the literary world. In some cases, where a definite talent is evidenced by the writer, they also accept as clients those who have had wide experience in the newspaper, and stage or radio fields. A comprehensive examination of the writer's credentials is made before the agency attempts to enter into any negotiations for a contract to represent him.

The writer who is not so well-known must choose a smaller agency to represent him. The small agencies operate on the same basis as the large ones, and are on the look-out at all times for new talent.

The writer should be very careful in the selection of his agent, since the studios deal only with recognized, reputable agencies.

The State of California and the State of New York have laws limiting the agency commission for the sale of literary material to 10 per cent of the selling price. There is no charge made to the client for the agent's efforts in trying to sell the story if no sale is made.

The larger agencies rarely, if ever, make any reading charges on manuscripts sent in to them by writers whom they have under contract. The reason for this is that the agency already has evidence of the ability of the author, and does not need to waste its time reading his material to discover if he can write. They know in advance that he has sufficient literary experience and ability to warrant the sales efforts of the agency.

The smaller agents, on the other hand, who have to handle the material submitted by the less experienced or less talented writer, must provide for some compensation for their time in reading the manuscripts to determine their acceptability, and their sales efforts in disposing of this material. The reading charge usually covers this.

It is common for such agencies to make a reasonable reading charge on at least the first few manuscripts submitted to them. Once they have made a sale to a studio of the writer's product, they do not, ordinarily, make any further charges for reading his manuscripts. Consequently, after the first sale is made, the writer need not trouble himself with the necessity of paying his representative for reading his material.

The writer should never, for his own protection, mail his story to any agency without determining in advance what charge will be made for reading his manuscript. After all arrangements have been made with the agent, and his manuscript is requested, then he may mail his story to the agent.

The Racketeer

Many stories are told in Hollywood of gullible amateurs falling into the hands of racketeers. Usually these amateurs do not know how to write even a decent letter. They know nothing of grammar and composition, and are absolutely ignorant of dramatic requirements. But they write stories—in some years they run into the hundreds of thousands. No legitimate agent will handle such stories.

What happens then is that the writer sends his "scenario"—usually the one and only copy he has, since it does not occur to him to make a carbon of his work—to some so-called agent, for reading. The "agent" then sends him back a glowing report, praising him for his wonderful story. The only fly in the ointment is, usually, that the story needs "rewriting" to make it just right for the screen. Will the amateur please send the "agent" the fee for changing his story into an epic? The "fee" is anywhere from ten dollars to whatever the traffic will bear—sometimes it runs into hundreds of dollars.

Another racket is to tell the amateur that, in order to protect his manuscript and to copyright it, he should have it "published." His story is then usually printed, along with those of other "suckers," in a pamphlet which nobody ever cares to see except the victims of this hoax. The writer has to pay anywhere from forty to several hundred dollars for this privilege. He is told that all the studios get a copy of the pamphlet—but if it ever reaches the studios it ends in the first wastebasket.

The amateur continues to send in his fee for changes, or for publication, in the hope that he will become a celebrity over night. The correspondence between the amateur and the racketeer may go on for months. But nothing ever happens. The studios have nothing to do with such racketeers. In fact, if a writer ever gets his story into such a publication, he is definitely marked as a nitwit.

The Better Business Bureau

While it is a practically hopeless task to convince any amateur that he is not a genius once he has fallen into the hands of the flattery artists who prey upon his gullibility, yet he must eventually wake up to cold reality when his cash runs low, and he gets no results for his money.

If there is any doubt in the writer's mind in regard to the agent with whom he may be doing business, he should communicate with the Better Business Bureau in Los Angeles, or in New York—wherever the agent happens to be located, to determine whether or not the terms which have been made to him by the agent are legal, and whether the agency has a good reputation.

Many writers have reported their troubles in the past few years to the Better Business Bureau, so that today that excellent organization has some worth-while data on the tricks of the racketeer in this business. A letter to the Bureau will ordinarily reveal quickly the status of the agent with whom the writer is doing business.

All in all, it is a good idea for any amateur writer to get in touch with the Better Business Bureau and to determine the reputation of his agent before he spends any money on having his story "rewritten."

CHAPTER XLV

EXPERIMENTS IN SCREEN WRITING

Many people believe they can write screen stories. Here is a way to prove it. An excellent test of one's ability is to adapt a book which is actually being used by the studios as the basis of a motion picture. A comparison between the writer's adaptation and the actual screen story which the studio has made out of the same book will reveal much.

The study might be undertaken by a group. The competition between the individuals of the group would bring out many ideas and twists to the basic idea and would stimulate considerable interest in plot development. The titles of books from which forthcoming films are being made can be obtained thru the medium of the movie columns in the newspapers and thru other sources of advance picture information.

The Book Synopsis

The book upon which the motion picture is being based should be read first from cover to cover. Then an outline should be made emphasizing the love interest, the conflict and the action suggested by the book. If the love interest seems to be lacking, then the synopsis should be prepared indicating the action and the conflict. When this is done the writer will have a book synopsis, which should give the skeleton of the plot and include only those incidents essential to plot motivation.

Screenplay Synopsis

After the book synopsis has been made, the story should be analyzed to determine its Code conformity, as follows:

1. What is the theme?
2. Is the theme allowable under the Code?
3. Is it a "problem" theme?
4. If it is a "problem" theme, does it have the necessary "compensating moral values" required by the Code?

If the story contains any problems which require special treatment under the Code, a second synopsis should be prepared, including the changes it has been necessary to introduce into the story to bring it into conformity with the Code.

After this synopsis has been made, the writer should see the picture which has been made from the book. He may find that many changes have been made in the film departing radically from the original story. However, these changes should not discourage him, since they merely serve to indicate the many developments possible in basic themes.

With the actual film for comparison, the writer can judge how close he has come to—or how far he has diverged from—the actual screenplay. The basic idea of the book and the film will usually be the same, but the plot may have been changed entirely in the film. On the other hand, one will find, occasionally, a screenplay which follows the original plot very closely.

Whatever the case may be the writer should proceed to analyze the original novel to determine what elements in the basic plot suggested the developments found in the screen version. Such a study will sharpen his dramatic sense, and at the same time, train the writer to think in terms of the screen, so that, after a few attempts, he may be able to develop the story in a way to parallel the screenplay. The third or fourth book which he synopsizes will be much better than the first two, for he will understand what to look for in the original story and what to develop in the screen plot.

The comparison of the novel and the screen play will indicate also how the Code has been applied in each case. If the picture differs from the writer's conception of the Code, then, without doubt, the writer needs to study the Code further; for the film—if it has been approved by the Production Code Administration—will always indicate the proper and correct application of the Code. To make certain that the film has been approved by the Production Code Administration, the writer should look for the seal of approval which appears in the lower left-hand corner on the title card of each picture which has been certified.

Where a competitive group undertakes such a study, there will be the advantage of comparison among the different members. Some one in the group will come pretty close to the screen story, and the rivalry for the next picture will add zest to the game. The members can discuss the story changes, Code applications, and the incidents in the original story which provided, or suggested, the plot development of the screen story.

APPENDICES

THE MOTION PICTURE PRODUCTION CODE OF 1930

FIRST SECTION

GENERAL PRINCIPLES

I. Theatrical motion pictures, that is, pictures intended for the theatre as distinct from pictures intended for churches, schools, lecture halls, educational movements, social reform movements, etc., are primarily to be regarded as *Entertainment.*

Mankind has always recognized the importance of entertainment and its value in rebuilding the bodies and souls of human beings.

But it has always recognized that entertainment can be of a character *harmful* to the human race, and, in consequence, has clearly distinguished between:

> *Entertainment which tends to improve* the race, or, at least, to recreate and rebuild human beings exhausted with the realities of life; and
>
> *Entertainment which tends to degrade human beings,* or to lower their standards of life and living.

Hence the *moral importance* of entertainment is something which has been universally recognized. It enters intimately into the lives of men and women and affects them closely; it occupies their minds and affections during leisure hours, and ultimately touches the whole of their lives. A man may be judged by his standard of entertainment as easily as by the standard of his work.

> So *correct entertainment raises* the whole standard of a nation.
>
> *Wrong entertainment lowers* the whole living condition and moral ideals of a race.

NOTE, for example, the healthy reactions to healthful moral sports like baseball, golf; the unhealthy reactions to sports like cockfighting, bullfighting, bear-baiting, etc. Note, too, the effect on a nation of gladiatorial combats, the obscene plays of Roman times, etc.

II. Motion pictures are very important as *Art*.

Though a new art, possibly a combination art, it has the same object as the other arts, the presentation of human thoughts, emotions and experiences, in terms of an appeal to the soul thru the senses.

Here, as in entertainment:

Art *enters intimately* into the lives of human beings.

Art can be *morally good*, lifting men to higher levels. This has been done thru good music, great painting, authentic fiction, poetry, drama.

Art can be morally evil in its effects. This is the case clearly enough with unclean art, indecent books, suggestive drama. The effect on the lives of men and women is obvious.

NOTE: It has often been argued that art in itself is unmoral, neither good nor bad. This is perhaps true of the *thing* which is music, painting, poetry, etc. But the thing is the *product* of some person's mind, and that mind was either good or bad morally when it produced the thing. And the thing has its *effect* upon those who come into contact with it. In both these ways, as a product and the cause of definite effects, it has a deep moral significance and an unmistakable moral quality.

HENCE: The motion pictures which are the most popular of modern arts for the masses, have their moral quality from the minds which produce them and from their effects on the moral lives and reactions of their audiences. This gives them a most important morality.

1) They *reproduce* the morality of the men who use the pictures as a medium for the expression of their ideas and ideals;

2) They *affect* the moral standards of those who thru the screen take in these ideas and ideals.

In the case of the motion pictures, this effect may be particularly emphasized because no art has so quick and so widespread an appeal to the masses. It has become in an incredibly short period, *the art of the multitudes.*

III. The motion picture has special *Moral obligations*:

A) Most arts appeal to the mature. This art appeals at once to every class—mature, immature, developed, undeveloped, law-abiding, criminal. Music has its grades for different classes; so has literature and drama. This art of the motion picture, combining as it does the two fundamental appeals of looking at a picture and listening to a story, at once reaches every class of society.

B) Because of the mobility of a film and the ease of picture distribution, and because of the possibility of duplicating positives in large quantities, this art *reaches places* unpenetrated by other forms of art.

C) Because of these two facts, it is difficult to produce films intended for only *certain classes of people.* The exhibitor's theatres are built for the masses, for the cultivated and the rude, mature and immature, self-restrained and inflammatory, young and old, law-respecting and criminal. Films, unlike books and music, can with difficulty be confined to certain selected groups.

D) The latitude given to film material cannot, in consequence, be as wide as the latitude given to *book material.* In addition:

(a) A book describes; a film vividly presents.

(b) A book reaches the mind thru words merely; a film reaches the eyes and ears thru the reproduction of actual events.

(c) The reaction of a reader to a book depends largely on the keenness of the reader; the reaction to a film depends on the vividness of presentation.

E) This is also true when comparing the film with the newspapers. Newspapers present by description, films by actual presentation. Newspapers are after the fact and present things that have taken place; the film gives the events in the process of enactment and with apparent reality of life.

F) Everything possible in a *play* is not possible in a film.
  (a) Because of the larger audience of the film, and its consequently mixed character. Psychologically, the larger the audience, the lower the moral mass resistance to suggestion.
  (b) Because thru light, enlargement of character presentation, scenic emphasis, etc., the screen story is brought closer to the audience than the play.
  (c) The enthusiasm for and interest in the film *actors* and *actresses,* developed beyond anything of the sort in history, makes the audience largely sympathetic toward the characters they portray and the stories in which they figure. Hence they are more ready to confuse the actor and character, and they are most receptive of the emotions and ideals portrayed and presented by their favorite stars.

G) Small communities, remote from sophistication and from the hardening process which often takes place in the ethical and moral standards of larger cities, are easily and readily reached by any sort of film.

H) The grandeur of mass meetings, large action, spectacular features, etc., affects and arouses more intensely the emotional side of the audience.

In general: The mobility, popularity, accessibility, emotional appeal, vividness, straight-forward presentation of fact in the films makes for intimate contact on a larger audience and greater emotional appeal.

Hence the larger moral responsibilities of the motion pictures.

Second Section

WORKING PRINCIPLES

I. No picture should lower the moral standards of those who see it. This is done:
  (a) When evil is made to appear *attractive,* and good is made to appear *unattractive.*
  (b) When the *sympathy* of the audience is thrown on the side of crime, wrong-doing, evil, sin.

The same thing is true of a film that would throw sympathy against goodness, honor, innocence, purity, honesty.

NOTE: *Sympathy with a person who sins,* is not the same as sympathy with the sin or crime of which he is guilty. We may feel sorry for the plight of the murderer or even understand the circumstances which led him to his crime; we may not feel sympathy with the wrong which he has done.

The presentation of evil is often essential for art, or fiction, or drama.

This in itself is not wrong, provided:

(a) That evil is *not presented alluringly.* Even if later on the evil is condemned or punished, it must not be allowed to appear so attractive that the emotions are drawn to desire' or approve so strongly that later they forget the condemnation and remember only the apparent joy of the sin.

(b) That thruout the presentation, *evil and good are never confused* and that evil is always recognized clearly as evil.

(c) That in the end the audience feels that *evil is wrong* and *good is right.*

II. Law, natural or divine, must not be belittled, ridiculed, nor must a sentiment be created against it.

A) The *presentation of crimes* against the law, human or divine, is often necessary for the carrying out of the plot. But the presentation must not throw sympathy with the criminal as against the law, nor with the crime as against those who must punish it.

B) The *courts* of the land should not be presented as *unjust.*

III. As far as possible, life should not be misrepresented, at least not in such a way as to place in the minds of youth false values on life.

NOTE: This subject is touched just in passing. The attention of the producers is called, however, to the magnificent possibilities of the screen for character development, the building of right ideals, the inculcation in story-form of right principles. If motion pictures consistently held up high types of character, presented stories that would affect lives for the better, they could become the greatest natural force for the improvement of mankind.

PRINCIPLES OF PLOT

In accordance with the general principles laid down:

1) No plot theme should definitely side *with evil and against good.*
2) Comedies and farces *should not make fun* of good, innocence, morality or justice.
3) No plot should be so constructed as to leave the question of *right or wrong in doubt or fogged.*
4) No plot should by its treatment *throw the sympathy* of the audience with sin, crime, wrong-doing or evil.
5) No plot should present *evil alluringly.*

Serious Film Drama

I.   As stated in the general principles, *sin and evil* enter into the story of human beings, and hence in themselves are dramatic material.

II. In the use of this material, it must be distinguished between *sin* which by its very nature *repels,* and *sin* which by its nature *attracts.*

    (a)   In the first class comes murder, most theft, most legal crimes, lying, hypocrisy, cruelty, etc.

    (b)   In the second class come sex sins, sins and crimes of apparent heroism, such as banditry, daring thefts, leadership in evil, organized crime, revenge, etc.

A)   The first class needs little care in handling, as sins and crimes of this class naturally are unattractive. The audience instinctively condemns and is repelled. Hence the one objective must be to avoid the *hardening* of the audiences, especially of those who are young and impressionable, to the thought and the fact of crime. People can become accustomed even to murder, cruelty, brutality and repellent crimes.

B)   The second class needs real care in handling, as the response of human natures to their appeal is obvious. This is treated more fully below.

III. A careful distinction can be made between films intended for *general distribution,* and films intended for use in theatres restricted to a *limited audience.* Themes and plots quite appropriate for the latter would be altogether out of place and dangerous in the former.

NOTE: In general, the practice of using a general theatre and limiting the patronage during the showing of a certain film to "adults only" is not completely satisfactory and is only partially effective.

However, maturer minds may easily understand and accept without harm subject matter in plots which does younger people positive harm.

HENCE: If there should be created a special type of theatre, catering exclusively to an adult audience, for plays of this character (plays with problem themes, difficult discussions and maturer treatment) it would seem to afford an outlet, which does not now exist, for pictures unsuitable for general distribution but permissible for exhibitions to a restricted audience.

PLOT MATERIAL

1) *The triangle,* that is, the love of a third party by one already married, needs careful handling, if marriage, the sanctity of the home, and sex morality are not to be imperilled.

2) *Adultery* as a subject should be avoided:

   (a) It is *never* a fit subject for *comedy.* Thru comedy of this sort, ridicule is thrown on the essential relationships of home and family and marriage, and illicit relationships are made to seem permissible, and either delightful or daring.

   (b) Sometimes adultery must be counted on as material occurring in serious drama.

   In this case:

   (1) It should not appear to be justified;

   (2) It should not be used to weaken respect for marriage;

   (3) It should not be presented as attractive or alluring.

3) *Seduction and rape* are difficult subjects and bad material from the viewpoint of the general audience in the theatre.

(a) They should never be introduced as subject matter *unless* absolutely essential to the plot.

(b) They should *never* be treated as comedy.

(c) Where essential to the plot, they must not be more than *suggested*.

(d) Even the struggles preceding rape should not be shown.

(e) The *methods* by which seduction, essential to the plot, is attained should not be explicit or represented in detail where there is likelihood of arousing wrongful emotions on the part of the audience.

4) *Scenes of passion* are sometimes necessary for the plot. However:

(a) They should appear only where necessary and *not* as an added stimulus to the emotions of the audience.

(b) *When not essential to the plot,* they should not occur.

(c) They must *not* be *explicit* in action nor vivid in method, e.g. by handling of the body, by lustful and prolonged kissing, by evidently lustful embraces, by positions which strongly arouse passions.

(d) In general, where essential to the plot, scenes of passion should *not* be presented in such a way as to *arouse or excite the passions of the ordinary spectator.*

5) *Sexual immorality* is sometimes necessary for the plot. It is subject to the following:

GENERAL PRINCIPLES—regarding plots dealing with sex, passion, and incidents relating to them:

All legislators have recognized clearly that there are in normal human beings emotions which react naturally and spontaneously to the presentation of certain definite manifestations of sex and passion.

(a) The presentation of scenes, episodes, plots, etc., which are deliberately meant to excite these manifestations on the part of the audience is always wrong, is subversive to the interest of society, and a peril to the human race.

(b) Sex and passion exist and consequently must *sometimes enter* into the stories which deal with human beings.

> (1) *Pure love,* the love of a man for a woman permitted by the law of God and man, is the rightful subject of plots. The passion arising from this love is not the subject for plots.

> (2) *Impure love,* the love of man and woman forbidden by human and divine law, must be presented in such a way that:
> > a) It is clearly known by the audience to be wrong;
> > b) Its presentation does not excite sexual reactions, mental or physical, in an ordinary audience;
> > c) It is not treated as matter for comedy.

HENCE: *Even within the limits of pure love,* certain facts have been universally regarded by lawmakers as outside the limits of safe presentation. These are the manifestations of passion and the sacred intimacies of private life:

> (1) Either before marriage in the courtship of decent people;

> (2) Or after marriage, as is perfectly clear.

In the case of pure love, the difficulty is not so much about what details are permitted for presentation. This is perfectly clear in most cases. The difficulty concerns itself with the tact, delicacy, and general regard for propriety manifested in their presentation.

But in the case of impure love, the love which society has always regarded as wrong and which has been banned by divine law, the following are important:

> (1) It must not be the subject of comedy or farce or treated as the material for laughter;

> (2) It must not be presented as attractive and beautiful;

(3) It must not be presented in such a way as to arouse passion or morbid curiosity on the part of the audience;

(4) It must not be made to seem right and permissible;

(5) In general, it must not be detailed in method or manner.

6) *The presentation of murder* is often necessary for the carrying out of the plot. However:

(a) Frequent presentation of *murder* tends to lessen regard for the sacredness of life.

(b) *Brutal killings* should not be presented in detail.

(c) *Killings for revenge* should not be justified, i.e., the hero should not take justice into his own hands in such a way as to make his killing seem justified. This does not refer to killings in self-defense.

(d) *Dueling* should not be presented as right or just.

7) *Crimes against the law* naturally occur in the course of film stories. However:

(a) *Criminals* should not be made heroes, even if they are historical criminals.

(b) *Law and justice* must not by the treatment they receive from criminals be made to seem wrong or ridiculous.

(c) *Methods of committing crime,* e.g., burglary, should not be so explicit as to teach the audience how crime can be committed; that is, the film should not serve as a possible school in crime methods for those who seeing the methods might use them.

(d) Crime need *not always be punished,* as long as the audience is made to know that it is wrong.

DETAILS
OF PLOT, EPISODE, AND TREATMENT

Vulgarity

Vulgarity may be carefully distinguished from obscenity. Vulgarity is the treatment of low, disgusting, unpleasant subjects which decent society considers outlawed from normal conversation.

Vulgarity in the motion pictures is limited in precisely the same way as in decent groups of men and women by the dictates of good taste and civilized usage, and by the effect of shock, scandal, and harm on those coming in contact with this vulgarity.

(1) *Oaths* should never be used as a comedy element. Where required by the plot, the less offensive oaths may be permitted.

(2) *Vulgar expressions* come under the same treatment as vulgarity in general. Where women and children are to see the film, vulgar expressions (and oaths) should be cut to the absolute essentials required by the situation.

(3) The name of *Jesus Christ* should never be used except in reverence.

Obscenity

Obscenity is concerned with immorality, but has the additional connotation of being common, vulgar and coarse.

(1) *Obscenity in fact,* that is, in spoken word, gesture, episode, plot, is against divine and human law, and hence altogether outside the range of subject matter or treatment.

(2) Obscenity should *not be suggested* by gesture, manner, etc.

(3) An obscene reference, even if it is expected to be understandable to only the more sophisticated part of the audience, should not be introduced.

(4) *Obscene language* is treated as all obscenity.

Costume

GENERAL PRINCIPLES:

(1) The effect of nudity or semi-nudity upon the normal man or woman, and much more upon the young person, has been honestly recognized by all lawmakers and moralists.

(2) Hence the fact that the nude or semi-nude body may be *beautiful* does not make its use in the films moral. For in addition to its beauty, the effects of the nude

or semi-nude body on the normal individual must be taken into consideration.

(3)   Nudity or semi-nudity used simply to put a "punch" into a picture comes under the head of immoral actions as treated above. It is immoral in its effect upon the average audience.

(4)   Nudity or semi-nudity is sometimes apparently necessary for the plot. *Nudity is never permitted.* Semi-nudity may be permitted under conditions.

PARTICULAR PRINCIPLES:

(1)   *The more intimate parts of the human body* are the male and female organs and the breasts of a woman.
(a)   They should *never be uncovered.*
(b)   They should *not* be covered with *transparent* or *translucent* material.
(c)   They should not be clearly and unmistakably *outlined* by the garment.

(2)   *The less intimate parts of the body,* the legs, arms, shoulders and back, are less certain of causing reactions on the part of the audience. Hence:
(a)   Exposure *necessary for the plot* or action is permitted.
(b)   Exposure *for the sake of exposure* or the "punch" is wrong.
(c)   *Scenes of undressing* should be avoided. When necessary for the plot, they should be kept within the limits of decency. When not necessary for the plot, they are to be avoided, as their effect on the ordinary spectator is harmful.
(d)   *The manner or treatment of exposure* should not be suggestive or indecent.
(e)   The following is important in connection with *dancing costumes:*
1.   Dancing costumes cut to permit *grace* or freedom of movement, provided they remain within the limits of decency indicated are permissible.
2.   Dancing costumes cut to *permit indecent actions* or movements or to make possible during the dance indecent exposure, are wrong, especially when permitting:
a)   Movements of the breasts;

   b) Movements of sexual suggestions of the
        intimate parts of the body;
   c) Suggestion of nudity.

Dancing

   (1) Dancing in general is recognized as an *art* and a
        beautiful form of expressing human emotion.
   (2) *Obscene dances are those*:
        (a) Which suggest or represent sexual actions,
             whether performed solo or with two or more;
        (b) Which are designed to excite an audience, to
             arouse passions, or to cause physical excitement.
        HENCE: Dances of the type known as "Kooch," or
                "Can-Can," since they violate decency in
                these two ways, are wrong.
                Dances with movements of the breasts, ex-
                cessive body movement while the feet remain
                stationary, the so-called "belly dances"—
                these dances are immoral, obscene, and hence
                altogether wrong.

Locations

Certain places are so closely and thoroly associated with
sexual life or with sexual sin that their use must be carefully
limited.

   (1) *Brothels and houses of ill-fame,* no matter of what
        country, are *not* proper locations for drama. They
        suggest to the average person at once sex sin, or they
        excite an unwholesome and morbid curiosity in the
        minds of youth.
        IN GENERAL: They are dangerous and bad dramatic
        locations.
   (2) *Bedrooms.* In themselves they are perfectly innocent.
        Their suggestion may be kept innocent. However,
        under certain conditions they are bad dramatic loca-
        tions.
        (a) Their use in a comedy or farce (on the principle
             of the so-called bedroom farce) is wrong, be-
             cause they suggest sex laxity and obscenity.
        (b) In serious drama, their use should, where sex
             is suggested, be confined to absolute essentials,
             in accordance with the principles laid down
             above.

Religion

    (1) No film or episode in a film should be allowed to *throw ridicule* on any religious faith honestly maintained.

    (2) *Ministers of religion* in their characters of ministers should not be used in comedy, as villains, or as unpleasant persons.

NOTE: The reason for this is not that there are not such ministers of religion, but because the attitude toward them tends to be an attitude toward religion in general.

Religion is lowered in the minds of the audience because it lowers their respect for the ministers.

    (3) *Ceremonies* of any definite religion should be supervised by someone thoroly conversant with that religion.

PARTICULAR APPLICATIONS OF THE CODE AND THE REASONS THERE-FOR [Addenda to 1930 Code]

GENERAL PRINCIPLES

[Brief re-statement]

1. No picture shall be produced which will lower the moral standards of those who see it. Hence the sympathy of the audience shall never be thrown to the side of crime, wrong-doing, evil or sin.

2. Correct standards of life, subject only to the requirements of drama and entertainment, shall be presented.

3. Law, natural or human, shall not be ridiculed, nor shall sympathy be created for its violation.

PARTICULAR APPLICATIONS

I. *Crimes against the law:*

These shall never be presented in such a way as to throw sympathy with the crime as against law and justice or to inspire others with a desire for imitation.

The treatment of crimes against the law must not:

    a. Teach methods of crime.

    b. Inspire potential criminals with a desire for imitation.

    c. Make criminals seem heroic and justified.

1. MURDER

    a. *The technique of murder* must be presented in a way that will *not* inspire imitation.

    b. *Brutal killings* are not to be presented in detail.

    c. *Revenge* in modern times shall not be justified. In lands and ages of less developed civilization and moral principles, revenge may sometimes be presented. This would be the case especially in places where no law exists to cover the crime because of which revenge is committed.

2. METHODS OF CRIME shall not be explicitly presented.
   a. *Theft, robbery, safe-cracking,* and *dynamiting* of trains, mines, buildings, etc., should not be detailed in method.
   b. *Arson* must be subject to the same safeguards.
   c. *The use of firearms* should be restricted to essentials.
   d. *Methods of smuggling* should not be presented.

3. ILLEGAL DRUG TRAFFIC must never be presented.
   Because of its evil consequences, the drug traffic should never be presented in any form. The existence of the trade should not be brought to the attention of audiences.

4. THE USE OF LIQUOR in American life, when not required by the plot or for proper characterization, should not be shown.
   The use of liquor should never be *excessively* presented even in picturing countries where its use is legal. In scenes from American life, the necessities of plot and proper characterization alone justify its use. And in this case, it should be shown with moderation.

II. *Sex*

The sanctity of the institution of marriage and the home shall be upheld. Pictures shall not infer that low forms of sex relationship are the accepted or common thing.

1. ADULTERY, sometimes necessary plot material, must not be explicitly treated, or justified, or presented attractively. Out of regard for the sanctity of marriage and the home, the *triangle,* that is, the love of a third party for one already married, needs careful handling. The treatment should not throw sympathy against marriage as an institution.

2. SCENES OF PASSION must be treated with an honest acknowledgment of human nature and its normal reactions. Many scenes cannot be presented without arousing dangerous emotions on the part of the immature, the young or the criminal classes.
   a. They should not be introduced when not essential to the plot.

b. Excessive and lustful kissing, lustful embraces, suggestive postures and gestures, are not to be shown.

c. In general, passion should be so treated that these scenes do not stimulate the lower and baser element.

3. SEDUCTION OR RAPE

a. They should never be more than suggested, and only when essential for the plot, and even then never shown by explicit method.

b. They are never the proper subject for comedy.

4. SEX PERVERSION or any inference to it is forbidden.

5. WHITE SLAVERY shall not be treated.

6. MISCEGENATION (sex relationship between the white and black races) is forbidden.

7. SEX HYGIENE AND VENEREAL DISEASES are not subjects for motion pictures.

8. SCENES OF ACTUAL CHILDBIRTH, in fact or in silhouette, are never to be presented.

9. CHILDREN'S SEX ORGANS are never to be exposed.

III. *Vulgarity*

The treatment of low, disgusting, unpleasant, though not necessarily evil, subjects should be subject always to the dictate of good taste and a regard for the sensibilities of the audience.

IV. *Obscenity*

Obscenity in word, gesture, reference, song, joke, or by suggestion (even when likely to be understood only by part of the audience) is forbidden.

V. *Profanity*

Pointed profanity (this includes the words, God, Lord, Jesus, Christ—unless used reverently—Hell, S.O.B., damn, Gawd), or every other profane or vulgar expression however used is forbidden.

VI. *Costume*

1. COMPLETE NUDITY is never permitted. This includes nudity in fact or in silhouette, or any lecherous or licentious notice thereof by other characters in the picture.

2. UNDRESSING SCENES should be avoided, and never used save where essential to the plot.
3. INDECENT OR UNDUE EXPOSURE is forbidden.
4. DANCING COSTUMES intended to permit undue exposure or indecent movements in the dance are forbidden.

VII. *Dances*

1. DANCES SUGGESTING OR REPRESENTING SEXUAL ACTIONS or indecent passion are forbidden.
2. DANCES WHICH EMPHASIZE INDECENT MOVEMENTS are to be regarded as obscene.

VIII. *Religion*

1. No FILM OR EPISODE MAY THROW RIDICULE on any religious faith.
2. MINISTERS OF RELIGION IN THEIR CHARACTER AS MINISTERS of religion should not be used as comic characters or as villains.
3. CEREMONIES OF ANY DEFINITE RELIGION should be carefully and respectfully handled.

IX. *Locations*

Certain places are so closely and thoroly associated with sexual life or with sexual sin that their use must be carefully limited. Brothels and houses of ill-fame are *not* proper locations for drama.

X. *National feelings*

The just rights, history, and feelings of any nation are entitled to consideration and respectful treatment.
1. The use of the Flag shall be consistently respectful.
2. The history, institutions, prominent people and citizenry of other nations shall be represented fairly.

XI. *Titles*

Salacious, indecent, or obscene titles shall not be used.

Appendix III

AMENDMENTS

   I. BRUTALITY, HORROR AND GRUESOME-
      NESS
  II. DRINKING
 III. GANGSTER STORIES
 IV. REGULATIONS RE CRIME IN MOTION PIC-
     TURES

NOTE: Rulings made by the Production Code Administration in the course of its work automatically become amendments to the Code. The regulation on drinking was necessary to indicate its manner of treatment after the repeal of Prohibition, since the original Code ruling had reference to Prohibition drinking.

I. *Brutality, horror and gruesomeness*

Scenes of excessive brutality and gruesomeness must be cut to an absolute minimum. Where such scenes, in the judgment of the Production Code Administration, are likely to prove seriously offensive, they will not be approved.

II. *Drinking in pictures*

"Drinking must be reduced to the absolute minimum essential for proper plot motivation."

The complaint is not so much against drinking when necessary for the plot, as, for instance, when a character is portrayed definitely as an unfortunate drunkard, or is driven to drink by circumstances inherent in the story. What is objected to is the incessant "smart" drinking apart from any story demands, or the exaggerated use of drinking for comedy .purposes.

III. *Gangster stories*

Crime stories are not acceptable when they portray the activities of American gangsters, armed and in violent conflict with the law or law-enforcing officers.

IV. *Regulations re crime in motion pictures*

   1. "Details of crime" must never be shown and care should be exercised at all times in discussing such details.

2. Action suggestive of wholesale slaughter of human beings, either by criminals, in conflict with police, or as between warring factions of criminals, or in public disorder of any kind, will not be allowed.

3. There must be no suggestion, at any time, of excessive brutality.

4. Because of the alarming increase in the number of films in which murder is frequently committed, action showing the taking of human life, *even in the mystery stories,* is to be cut to the minimum. These frequent presentations of murder tend to lessen regard for the sacredness of life.

5. Suicide, as a solution of problems occurring in the development of screen drama, is to be discouraged as "morally questionable" and as "bad theatre"—unless absolutely necessary for the development of the plot.

6. There must be no display at any time, of *machine guns, sub-machine guns* or other weapons generally classified as illegal weapons, in the hands of gangsters, or other criminals, and there are to be no off-stage sounds of the repercussion of these guns. This means that even where the machine guns, or other prohibited weapons, are *not* shown, the effect of shots coming from these guns must be *cut to a minimum.*

7. There must be no new, unique or "trick" methods for concealing of guns shown at any time.

8. The flaunting of weapons by gangsters, or other criminals, will not be allowed.

9. All discussions and dialogue on the part of gangsters regarding guns should be cut to the minimum.

10. There must be no scenes, at any time, showing law-enforcing officers dying at the hands of criminals. This includes private detectives, and guards for banks, motor trucks, etc.

11. With special reference to the crime of kidnaping—or illegal abduction—it has been our policy to mark such stories as acceptable under the Code *only* when the kidnaping or abduction is (a) not the main theme of the story; (b) the person kidnaped is not a child; (c) there are no "details of the crime" of kidnaping; (d) no profit accrues to the abductors or kidnapers; and (e) where the kidnapers are punished.

LIST OF LITERARY AGENTS

The following are a few of the well-known agents in Hollywood. Additional names may be secured by referring to the sources indicated on pages 261-2.

Adeline Alvord, 6605 Hollywood Boulevard, Hollywood.

Bachmann-Herzbrun, Inc., 9000 Sunset Boulevard, Hollywood.

Phil Berg-Bert Allenberg, Inc., 9494 Wilshire Boulevard, Beverly Hills.

Collier & Wallace, 7046 Hollywood Boulevard, Hollywood

Edington & Vincent, 6253 Hollywood Boulevard, Hollywood.

Freddie Fralick, 9016 Sunset Boulevard, Hollywood.

Hawkes-Volck Corp., 9441 Wilshire Boulevard, Beverly Hills.

Kingston & Meyers, Inc., 9120 Sunset Boulevard, Hollywood.

Lichtig & Englander, 405 Warner Theatre Bldg., Hollywood.

Wm. Morris Agency, Inc., 1680 N. Vine St., Hollywood.

Orsatti & Co., 9121 Sunset Boulevard, Hollywood.

Selznick & Joyce, 9460 Wilshire Boulevard, Beverly Hills.

Small-Landau Company, 6331 Hollywood Boulevard, Hollywood.

Zanft-Evans, Ltd., 8782 Sunset Boulevard, Los Angeles.

INDEX